BABY TALK

BABY TALK

The Secret Diary of A Pregnant Woman

by
Julie Walters, aged 37½

cartoons by
Maurice Dodd

EBURY PRESS
London

First published in 1990 by Ebury Press
an imprint of the Random Century Group
Random Century House
20 Vauxhall Bridge Road
London SW1V 2SA

Second impression 1990
Third impression 1990
Fourth impression 1990
Fifth impression 1990
Sixth impression 1990

British Library Cataloguing in Publication Data
Walters, Julie
    Baby talk.
    1. Great Britain. Women. Pregnancy & childbirth
    I. Title
    618.2'00941

    ISBN 0–85223–767–7

Typeset in Century Old Style by Textype Typesetters, Cambridge
Printed and bound by Mackays of Chatham, PLC

For Maisie
and of course
for Grant

CONTENTS

THE DECISION

4 December 1986

Two years ago tonight I was having a girls' night out in a local wine bar with my best pal, Ros. My memory of the evening is dim, due to the old drink (in this case, white wine that would have been better employed removing nail varnish), and is peopled mainly by shadowy figures often whispering, 'Is that Tracy Ullman?'

One of these shadows, a tall one with a deep voice, who had not asked this question, offered to walk us both home as he lived locally and feared for what might become of us if we were left to our own devices. When we reached my door after dropping Ros off, I invited him for a cup of something. At first he declined, but after I'd assured him that I wouldn't interfere with him and that he was quite safe, he accepted.

I remember almost nothing of what happened subsequently, and the next point at which my memory picks up the story I was standing in the kitchen looking down at the back of this friendly shadow while he inspected my broken washing machine. He then murmured something about me needing a pump. At the time I mistook his meaning and, instantly filled with mischief and glee, I took a running jump and sprang several feet in the air, landing on his back like a bareback rider in a circus. He, thinking he was being attacked, stood up and tried to remove me. I wasn't having

any of it. I clung on round his neck like a limpet and, laughing drain-like, I declared, 'I want you to have my children! It's right! I feel it in my ovaries.'

The next day, waves of embarrassment continually washed over me as snippets of the activities of the night before popped into my consciousness. One of the worst was the memory of his telling me his age (twenty-eight) and me replying loudly, and with awful arrogance, 'Oh, you're just a boy. I'm a woman of thirty-five. I'm in my prime. You couldn't even begin to make love to me.' As far as I knew, he hadn't wanted to.

I hoped with all my heart that I wouldn't bump into him in the street and, catching a glimpse in the mirror of my hung-over face, looking all of seventy-one, that 'hoped' became an absolute 'must not'. However, I did. He phoned and then came round. I almost didn't recognize him and was thrilled to find he was so handsome. I'd obviously got better taste drunk than sober. He came round to have lunch, and has been here ever since. . . .

This time last year while we were on holiday in Corsica we decided to have Maisie. It just seemed that the time was right. I felt I had spent thirty-seven years more or less solely concerned with myself, my relationships, my career, my this, my that. It had been great, I had reaped many benefits from it and now I wanted to give. 'Give what?' I asked myself at the time. Well, I suppose Life is the answer, and Love, plus the space for that life to be lived to the fullest. I can't put it into words – it just seemed right.

Grant would be a great dad, I decided. He is very responsible, totally reliable, strong, gentle, kind and unutterably practical. Mind you, I wouldn't have considered having a baby with him if he was anything else. I go cold at the thought of some of the horror stories our cleaner, Benita, told me. Her husband is Grant's opposite – totally inept in almost every field. He wouldn't know how to wash a sock. She came in one day to find him picking bits of glass out of her baby daughter's head. He had, in an unusual display of affection, thrown her into the air so that she had head-butted the light bulb. Another time, having returned from a visit to his mother's, he removed the carrycot plus baby from the car and placed it on the car roof, after which he got the Sunday papers out. A moment or so later he decided he was parked rather badly. He turned the engine on, then remembered the baby on the roof and slipped his foot off the clutch. The car duly jolted forward, knocking over a stone urn full of geraniums that adorned their front path. Meantime, the carrycot had shot forward down the windscreen, turning over and toppling the baby on to the bonnet. Benita's husband slept in the garage that night....

I just knew without question that Grant would make a wonderful dad. I couldn't tolerate a man who was domestically inept – the 'Why isn't my dinner on the table?' variety. Such a lot of women have to bring up their husbands as well as their children. Grant is able to cook, wash and sew probably better than me, and he doesn't see it as a slur on his masculinity. He wanted this baby as much as I did and the responsibility was always going to be completely shared. The old ovaries were right. 'Happy anniversary, mate!' I thought.

11 June 1987

Today I hung up my cap, metaphorically speaking. My Dutch cap.

I can't say I was sad to see it put away in its little neat box in the bathroom cabinet. It had always been chiefly a source of discomfort and embarrassment right from the start when I first had it fitted in a London clinic. It was to be a new experience and not one I relished the thought of. I was squeamish, to say the least, about introducing an alien piece of rubber into the temple of my spirit, my body.

Once inside the surgery, the nurse – a friendly type in a Brown Owlish sort of way – assured me there was nothing to fear. She asked me to remove my underwear and hop on the couch. Then she began an internal examination.

'Just relax,' she said.

I'm sorry, but I find relaxation completely incompatible with having a metal object looking just like the vicious beak of a large bird inserted into my Mary Jane. However, a girl does her best, and when the ordeal was over, and after several probings with a gloved hand in which she almost lost her fingers, the nurse opened a drawer and produced a rubber, dome-shaped thing. Announcing, 'This looks like your size', she advanced towards me.

My size? It was straight out of *Star Wars* and enormous! 'Where are you going to put it?' I asked with growing trepidation. 'On my head? It'll fall down over my ears!'

'Don't be silly,' she said. 'You've got plenty of room.'

Before I knew it, with frightening efficiency she had it installed. It felt fine, and with equal speed and efficiency she removed it and, holding it out to me, said, 'Now you try.'

With that, she whisked a set of screens around me and left me to perform this unnatural act alone.

'Squat and then insert it,' she suggested from the other side.

The squatting part was the easy bit. The inserting was obviously going to take a little longer, for the slippery little doings shot from my grip and went sailing through the air like a miniature UFO, to be caught, more through luck than skill, in my other hand. As my fingers closed around it, off it went again, launched into the atmosphere and again landing in the opposite hand. I imagined for a moment achieving this with several Dutch caps and starting a nightclub act. Finally, I managed the insertion and, upon instruction from Brown Owl, attempted its removal. I couldn't find it. Panicked fingers scrabbled frantically for a touch of rubber, but to no avail. At first I thought that, perhaps mistakenly, I'd put it in the wrong place. Impossible. I checked – it wasn't there, either.

Brown Owl came to the rescue. Before you could say, 'KY jelly', the gloved hand was there. But suddenly, as she was deftly checking that its position was correct, all activity ceased.

I shifted my gaze from the ceiling, where I had fixed it to make me relax, to find she was staring at me with an expression I simply couldn't fathom. In mid-pelvic examination she said, in a ponderous voice, 'I know you, don't I?'

'In what way?' I asked, thinking that she might mean gynaecologically, but suspecting she didn't.

Slowly she removed the cap and, still staring, pointed at me with it and, pleased as punch, said, 'Lenny Henry!'

I thought, surely to God she can't be confusing me with a black male comedian? However brilliant Lenny is, I couldn't pretend to be flattered. Then, by means of an explanation, she added, 'You did an act with him.' The penny depressingly dropped.

'No! No, I'm not Tracy Ullman,' I said. But with the surety of a pantomime audience, she replied, 'Oh yes, you are!'

The cap was pretty depressing all round, really, but not half as depressing as my first brush with contraception, the Pill. I was optimistically using it for a year before losing my virginity. It was one of those dangerous pills with too much oestrogen – at the beginning of each month I would wake every morning mildly irritated, and by the end of each month I wanted to smash every breakable object in the house. And

I could never take condoms seriously after the experience as a toddler of finding one of Daddy's special balloons under my parents' bed and taking it in turns with a small friend to blow it up. I never was taken with the smell of hot rubber, anyway. So the old cap is probably the best of a bad lot.

26 August 1987

I'm officially expecting a baby. Brilliant! I knew I must be because this morning I was sick. Our tom-cat, instead of bringing home birds and mice, is in the habit of forcing his way through the cat flap with anything from McDonald's milkshake cartons to other people's floorcloths. But today, waiting to greet me in the middle of the kitchen floor at 7 a.m. was a condom. An old condom. I stared at it, thinking that the cat must have some psychic powers and was forecasting my condition, when suddenly the glass of grape juice I'd drunk in the small hours was transferred to the kitchen walls in a Ralph Steadman-like SPLAT!

Apparently my genius child will make its entrance into the world, and devastate mine, on 10 May. Having worked out the approximate dates of conception, it seems it happened on holiday. This means she was made in Hong Kong.

It's still a miracle to me really that I've got this far. When I was three years old I saw my father, wearing only a pyjama top, get out of bed and put on a dressing gown. I knew I'd seen a lot of dark hair where his jacket ended and his pyjama bottoms should have begun, but I could have sworn there was something else. _Extra. Dangling._ Or was it just a trick of the light? As my father had never mentioned such an appendage, I thought it best to tackle my mother on this one.

Whilst pushing tangled sheets through the mangle, she put me straight. I'd asked, pointing to the appropriate place, 'Is

Daddy the same as me?' She immediately whipped her head away from me, apparently to look at something in next door's garden, and with obvious irritation, but very firmly, answered, 'YEEES!' This, I must admit, was a relief, because I hadn't liked the look of what I'd seen one bit. It also meant that what I'd *definitely* seen when my brother was in the bath would drop off in time and he'd get better.

Generally speaking, the topic of sex when discussed with my mother in my childhood was always riddled with embarrassed evasion and delusion. During my early schooldays the resultant bundle of misunderstandings was compounded by the nuns, who informed us mysteriously that chocolate was a stimulant and therefore to be avoided, that patent leather shoes were not to be worn for fear of their reflecting a girl's nether regions and, odder still, that no girl must cross her legs because you never saw the Virgin Mary cross hers. I personally have never seen the Virgin Mary cross anything.

And so it was with great ignorance that I entered puberty. I didn't even realize that I had a vagina. This was not helped by the loss of my virginity, a process so lengthy and so painful that I thought, 'Oh, I see, the man actually has to make the hole by pounding away with his penis.'

Well, I eventually sorted all this out and, to prove it, my doctor has confirmed that at thirty seven and a half years of age I am expecting a baby. Grant and I are totally thrilled and it was very much planned and hoped for, but as we drove away from the doctor's, high on our news, my heart went cold. My mother would have to be told and what, seconds ago, was an announcement I was bursting to make to the world became a confession I was absolutely dreading. I was sixteen again. The schoolgirl who'd made a mistake behind the bike sheds. AN UNMARRIED MOTHER about to have AN ILLEGITIMATE BABY. How can I ever pick up the phone? I can't, I'm going to write.

2 September 1987

I thought morning sickness was a little mild queasiness experienced first thing in the morning. For some women, yes. For me, not a bit of it. In fact, I have renamed it 'vile, unrelenting, morning, noon and night sickness'.

It began about a week ago with periodic attacks of nausea and has progressed daily to fit the above description. This has made life very difficult as I am at the moment rehearsing for the film *Buster* with Phil Collins and I have been instructed by the producer not to breathe a word about my condition, not even to Phil. What he must make of my sudden and very frequent lurchings to the lavatory, God alone knows, especially as the first of these occurred during a very intimate love scene. 'I love you, Junie,' he said with conviction and passion.

'I louargh....' Instead of the loving, romantic, reply my throat was filled with the dreaded sickness and the first of many exits was made.

With each of these my paranoia grows, because in order to reach the ladies I have to pass the production office, the door of which is always open. It is occupied by two women on typewriters, both of whom have an excellent view of anyone passing. At first they barely looked up, but by the end of the day they were positively waiting for me, staring each time with growing curiosity. One time as I staggered by, my face the colour of an avocado, I swear I heard the word 'drugs' mentioned.

__9 September 1987__

Today, the above-mentioned appalling condition reached a horrible crescendo. I was in a London cab on my way to see Mr P, the obstetrician. We were progressing down Wigmore Street when it started. Beads of sweat spread on my brow as I went into a panic of foreboding. I quickly searched my pocket, my handbag, frantically scrabbling for tissues and anything, anything resembling a receptacle. Too late! Eggs, bacon, beans and tomatoes (there are always tomatoes) sprayed like a modern abstract painting over windows, doors and foldaway seat.

The cab screeched to a halt, throwing me and the contents of my handbag against the aforesaid artwork. For a split second I did wonder if there was a little method in the cabbie's madness, as the sleeve of my new linen jacket had wiped the window clean. The glass partition shot open. As this book may be read by those experiencing the delicate and sensitive condition of pregnancy, I won't relate the driver's exact words, but 'Oh my God! I don't believe it!', uttered with a mixture of menace and world-weariness, was peppered with several colourful descriptions of my own good self.

He then went into a nearby shop, leaving me shaking and ashamed. He returned some minutes later with a steaming bucket of hot water and a toilet roll. He handed me the latter, then ordered me on to the pavement with a very loud 'OUT!' I stood there weakly mopping myself while he sluiced out the inside of the cab.

Like a naughty child I was then ordered back in, and I apologized almost continuously for the rest of the journey. What happened next was to push my embarrassment to levels as yet beyond my experience. We arrived at my destination and I got out my purse to pay. I found, to my

surprise, that the notes inside were soaking wet. To my further surprise – and horror – I found that the little bottle containing my urine sample was empty, the top nowhere to be seen. I still had the toilet roll and I dried a tenner as best I could. The cabbie took it silently with a look of hatred mingled with distaste, and if right then he didn't know the reason for the tenner's wetness, he soon would, for as he drove off I saw him clipping it to the dashboard, just above his heater....

__10 September 1987__

The letter I've been waiting for from my mother arrived today. I opened it with a racing heart. She was pleased, and concerned for my health.

I'm thirty-seven-and-a-half again.

__15 September 1987__

I have taken the decision to go private. It was difficult, because I am a total believer in the National Health Service and I deplore what Thatcher's government is doing to it. My decision was partly, if not wholly, based on an experience I had in 1983, when all the hoo-ha about *Educating Rita* was at its height.

It was when I was forced to go into hospital because of severe back pain which might have been, but turned out not to be, a kidney stone. It all started by me being transported, ashen-faced in a pool of sweat and paralysing discomfort, by ambulance to hospital. I remember the trip only as a blur of pain punctuated by one unforgettable event. The ambulance man, who was otherwise wonderful, ASKED ME FOR MY

AUTOGRAPH. Hardly able to remain conscious, I obliged.

On the ward I was surrounded by twenty-odd pairs of eyes viewing me as if I had several heads, and it was perhaps best to keep their distance. Patients who had to pass my bed to go to the toilet would, on approaching it, take a detour around the flower arrangements and avert their eyes as if I were dead or radioactive. Those who were up and about often grouped together to stare and talk loudly about me as though I were totally deaf or blind, or simply not there. As if I was there on TV.

They discussed my work, what they liked or didn't like, whether in their opinion I was funny, the fact that I was wearing a hospital nightie and the fact that I was going to the toilet rather a lot. Luckily, I was flanked by two old Nellies – two very old ladies both called Nelly – neither of whom had any idea who I was. The poor old soul on the left persistently called out for Sydney and, thinking she was at home, kept trying to get up to get the tea ready. This was forbidden, due to the fact that she had two broken ankles. However,

every ten minutes she diligently made an attempt. As this was a huge ward of thirty-two patients, many of whom needed heavy nursing care, and with just a couple of overworked and knackered nurses on duty, I felt it was my duty to get up and prevent old Nelly doing herself 'damage'.

After several days of my efforts she took me by the arm, looked me steadily in the eye and, in a rare moment of lucidity and with some irritation, cried, 'Look, do I owe you money?' Nelly was a treat and we started to get quite close, in a doolally sort of way.

Nelly had nothing to do with my decision to go private. What probably did swing it was waking from a heavy, pethidine-induced sleep on my first afternoon to find a total stranger sitting next to my bed. He said his name was Dave and that he'd read in the paper I was here in hospital and he'd thought he'd come to be 'a bit of company for me' as I was in a strange town.

I was in agony, and I can't say that his 'bit of company' two hours every afternoon for a week, with his barrage of questions like 'What's it like to work with Michael Caine?', 'How did you get into acting?' and 'What are you doing next?', was in any way welcome.

On some afternoons this man, who was bordering on the lunatic, would bring an equally mad companion who would ask me more or less the same questions. There was no way that I could ask this sadly understaffed ward to provide a vetting service to protect me from the local loonies, so I put up with it until the day he brought yet another retarded-looking friend – and a camera. I was photographed with him. With his friend. The nurse took all three of us. Then we had the nurse, him and me, and finally his friend, the nurse and me. During this photo session a genuine friend poked his head round the ward door, saw the carryings on and mouthed, 'I'll come back tonight.'

I was boiling with rage inside, at which point Dave's dumb friend asked, 'What will you be doing next?'

I answered, eyes full of hatred, 'I'll be strangling you, if you don't leave now.' To cap it all, I heard the little group of 'up-and-abouts' opposite refer to loopy Dave as what they thought might be 'the boyfriend'. I wouldn't have minded but he wore flares.

I quite understand the patients' attitudes concerning me. It's difficult to behave normally towards a person you feel familiar with because of television and the media, and yet don't know personally. I once found myself alone in a lift with Andrew Gardner. I stared at him, blushed, and announced to an empty space next to me, 'It's the man who reads the news.' I then laughed nervously. He looked quite frightened.

When a person is well and in control of their everyday life, being recognized is easily coped with and part of the job, so to speak. But when you're ill or when you're going to give birth, you realize how wonderfully private anonymity is, and how important.

___17 September 1987___

Today I had make-up and hair tests somewhere in Soho for a possible commercial. The hairdresser, Linda, under instructions to make me look pretty and natural with a variety of wigs, found several interesting and very different ways of making me look like Myra Hindley.

While she was achieving this, part of me was thinking, 'Oh, I really must say something', while the rest of me was engaged in a discussion with the make-up artist about natural childbirth. She, in a challenging and overbearing way, was all for it. Anything else was unfair on the child and she had no time for hospitals.

'The child should be born where it was conceived,' she said with authority.

'I don't think I'd feel safe giving birth on our kitchen table,' I replied. 'It's got a wobbly leg.'

'Oh, trust *you* to make light of it,' she said.

I said, 'Yes, I was only joking. We can't afford a trip back to Hong Kong. And besides, I can't remember what the number of the hotel room was.'

With that, she swanned silently out of the room.

I turned my attention back to the mirror. Linda's creation was coming along apace. The reflection staring back at me was that of a poor soul whose hair had fallen out years before and who'd had to resort to a National Health wig. I opened my mouth to protest when Linda piped up, in a Lancashire accent that made Bet Lynch sound like the Queen:

'I'd pay for a Caesarian, me. When our Lauren's 'ead were coomin' out, I were screamin' "Put it back! For Christ's sake, put it back!" And afterwards, you'd never think sitting down could be such a torture. I've never been right in that department since. I'm sure that's why we don't get on now.'

She then extolled the virtues of the Caesar. How you were cut in a far more civilized place below the bikini line and how the scar soon disappeared. But even that had its hazards. She went on to describe how a very famous actress's pubic hair had fallen out and that she, Linda, had had to have something called a mirkin made for her so that she could appear naked in a film.

Now, I'd seen this word 'mirkin' in the BBC's wig department on a cardboard box. It was next to another box which had '*Henry V*' written on it, so I'd assumed that the contents of

the former were a number of small goatee beards. Well, now I know better. And I regret putting them on my chin!

18 September 1987

The costume designer on *Buster* really must be told of my pregnancy. She came round today to do a second fitting. Having only fitted me a couple of weeks ago, she visibly blanched when she saw that the 1960s' bra that she had brought, and which had fitted me perfectly when first tried on, was now bulging with twin monsters. She was speechless with embarrassment as we both stared at my mammoth bosom. She then uttered a very small 'Oh!' and I tried on some clothes.

Nothing quite fitted as it had. The neat little two-piece that I'd so loved was now gaping between its buttons, and I looked as if I'd been shop-lifting melons. As I changed back into my clothes I caught her staring at my bosom, obviously looking for tell-tale signs of silicone implants. I could stand it no longer and the word 'pregnant' exploded into the silence, unaccompanied by any other word. She looked flummoxed for a moment and then, with dawning realization, said, 'Oh, thank goodness for that.'

___24 September 1987___

The morning sickness continues unabated, catching me out any time, anywhere, and with little warning. Today, at least I had one consolation. The wonderful vegetable curry I had for lunch was savoured twice – going down and then coming back up. During the latter event it almost tasted better.

___30 September 1987___

I hereby warn all pregnant persons reading this diary that they will be inundated with birth-related horror stories. People will, without any invitation whatsoever, recount in the most lurid detail the experiences of mothers, sisters, daughters, friends and friends of friends.

Today was the turn of my accountant. I wouldn't have minded but I'd rung up about my VAT!

He said that a friend of his knew someone who in the latter stages of pregnancy was suffering from appalling wind, accompanied by a lot of discomfort in the lower region. A few days prior to the estimated date of delivery this discomfort was particularly bad, so the woman in question, feeling that a bowel movement was imminent, went off to the lav. After what she thought was a rather difficult evacuation she

stood up and, on turning round, found the baby virtually sitting in the lavatory bowl!

I thanked my accountant for this titbit and said I would bear it in mind. I am none the wiser on my VAT problem but I will leave it for another day!

___2 October 1987___

My VAT problem could not wait a second longer, so today I rang my accountant again to sort it out. He saw this as an opportunity to regale me with yet another blood-curdling story. This time it was the wife of a friend of his who was going to have a Caesarian. It seemed that the night prior to the op she dreamt that, although there was a screen across her abdomen to block her view of everything, the surgeon wore glasses and every grisly detail was perfectly reflected in them! The next day, when the actual event took place, to her horror the surgeon really *did* wear glasses, so she relived the awful experience again, only this time for real.... He told me this with great glee.

After a short period of speechlessness, I thanked him and said that *were* I to have a Caesarian, and *if* Mr P wore his glasses, I would remember to avert my eyes.

Phone calls to my accountant seem to be turning into a sort of obstetric *Tales of the Unexpected*.

___5 October 1987___

Horror of horrors! Today I threw up on the KINGS ROAD! I was being driven home by the unit car which was not inconspicuous, being a huge white Mercedes. I flung the door open at a set of traffic lights and my lunchtime lasagne landed

on a Ford Fiesta which had just pulled up alongside. It's funny – the driver's words were almost identical to those of the cab driver in Wigmore Street....

My driver sorted things out, somehow. I heard vague mutterings about my state of health, and as we were pulling away the Fiesta man asked, 'Is that Tracy Ullman?'

'Say yes!' I hissed from the back seat. This has got to be the worst day of my life.

___11 October 1987_____

Twelve weeks – there's good news and bad news.

Good news first. Dead on twelve weeks, just like all the textbooks say, the morning sickness has stopped. The only sign that it was ever there is that I can't bear the thought of tea, coffee or alcohol.

The bad news is that Mr P announced today that it would be advisable for me to have an amniocentesis. This has come as a bit of a blow as I was certain the old amnio was outmoded and had been replaced by a simple urine test. I was sure I'd seen it on *Tomorrow's World*. So sure was I that when a well-meaning friend of mine suggested not long ago that I might need one, I pooh-poohed the idea and told her of this new test.

'Oh, lucky you,' she said, and proceeded to tell me, in scary detail, about her experience of the amnio.

'The needle was this big, no kidding,' she said, holding her hands at least a foot apart. 'And really thick. And when the doctor put it in, the pain was awful and I felt the baby jump away from the needle. Then afterwards I had a series of really painful contractions.'

Her description is at this moment zinging around my head along with the fact that there is a one-in-a-hundred chance of miscarriage. Mr P says amniocentesis must be carried out at sixteen weeks and it will detect many deformities in the foetus, but mainly Down's syndrome and spina bifida. He says the chances of incurring these sorts of problems at my age are much higher than they would have been even two years ago.

The test is carried out by inserting a needle into the womb and drawing off some amniotic fluid – the fluid the baby thrives in. This apparently can be done quite safely by using a scan to detect the exact position of the baby. The chromosomes are then taken off and grown in laboratory conditions, and this is when any abnormalities will show up. Also, the sex of the baby will be revealed. I'm not looking forward to this process and in fact would rather have my head removed.

____12 October 1987____

At last I've been told it's OK to tell Phil I'm pregnant. I must say this was a tremendous relief. I was longing to explain what must have appeared to be my slightly quirky behaviour, why I turned green when people put a cup of tea in front of me, why I slept if I had more than ten minutes off in between shots, why these enormous bosoms had replaced my pre- viously rather modest set and why Annie, my stand-in, was always hovering with a chair and with something to put my feet upon. Come to think of it, the latter must have appeared cringe-makingly starry.

We were on location by the Thames on the South Bank and Phil was sitting in his car with his driver, Danny. I banged on the window and mouthed, 'Can I get in?'

They both mouthed back, 'Sure', and in I got.

'Phil, I've got something to tell you,' I said, my voice

strident with excitement. 'I'm pregnant.' I quickly realized it must have sounded like a paternity suit was being issued and added, 'It's OK, I'm not a greedy girl, I'm sure we can come to some reasonable financial arrangement.'

He laughed and was thrilled for us both – Grant and me, that is. Danny too was pleased and congratulated me, adding, 'If the press find out you'll think I'm the grass.'

Laughing, I said, 'Don't be silly.'

When I was dropped off this evening I noticed there was a small, dishevelled-looking man sitting on the wall opposite our house. I instantly recognized him as a reporter, not because of his dress or stature but by his lurking nature and the fact that it was a dark night and his face appeared to be illuminated by his nose. I slipped into the house before he could catch me and he periodically banged on the door for two hours before sloping off. On the answerphone was a message from a journalist I knew who said she had heard from a reliable source that I was pregnant and congratulations.

___13 October 1987___

Sure enough today, there it was, on the front page of one of the tabloids. But it was a nice piece so I didn't mind, even though there was an actual quote from me and I hadn't spoken to anyone and the photograph alongside it made me look like I should never go anywhere near children.

Just before I left for filming around mid-morning, there was a bang on the door. Thinking there was no longer a story I unsuspectingly opened it, and there was the lurking little man with the navy blue nose and next to him in a rather deep hole in the pavement was a British Telecom man. Old blue nose looked me directly in the eye and said, 'Does Julie Walters live here?'

I said, 'No, no, not that I know of.'

Just then, totally uninvited, the British Telecom man chimed in, 'No, that's not Julie Walters, you daft sod', gave me a quick wink and carried on with his wires.

'I could have sworn she lived here,' blue nose persisted.

'Naw, mate, you got it wrong,' the British Telecom man assured him, and disappointed blue nose sloped off again.

I was just about to thank the BT man for helping to hoodwink the hack when he said, 'Do you often get taken for Julie Walters? Actually, I think you look more like Tracy Ullman.'

Thrilled, I went off to work.

P.S. Just to set the story straight, Danny was not the grass – but he was ribbed heavily about it for the rest of the film.

___5 November 1987___

I woke this morning laden with dread, my head full of images of enormous syringes piercing taut abdomens and going straight into the head of the tiny foetus and killing it stone dead. This pleasant little scenario played itself through whenever my mind unwittingly gave it space, so it was almost a relief to find myself lying on a bed in the hospital, with a kindly doctor telling me everything was going to be all

right and that first of all we would have a look at a scan.

I had had one of these earlier, at eight weeks, and so I knew what to expect. But what I was totally unprepared for was the miraculous development in just eight weeks from a minute throbbing mass of cells to a tiny little person, somersaulting around at a rate of knots and putting on what can only be described as a real show. The baby then settled down to sleep, endearingly curled up with its back to the camera. Apparently at this stage they alternately have ten minutes of activity and ten minutes of sleep.

I was so enthralled and overwhelmed that all this was going on inside me without my knowledge, and that the baby's basic chassis had already been assembled, that the amnio passed without any trauma whatsoever. I experienced no pain and had no anaesthetic. In fact, immediately afterwards I went off for a blood test and that was more painful.

I'm going to kill that well-meaning friend!

___23 November 1987___

I have now been in Acapulco a week to complete the shooting of *Buster*. The view from the suite is sensational, overlooking Acapulco Bay and the Pacific Ocean. The view from the side, however, is over the dustbins and the square of concrete used by an ill-assorted group of dancers who appear to be working out some sort of appalling disco number to the highly tedious Top Twenty hit 'La Bamba'.

This has been going on every day for several hours and I wish they'd hurry up and get it sorted out because I've run out of missiles to hurl. I have now lost one pair of sandals, several coathangers and a copy of *Hollywood Wives*. Grant has lost one flip-flop and one trainer, and the hotel has lost a flannel a day (wet), a grapefruit, four bananas and an apple from the courtesy hamper left for us by the manager. So now there's only the pineapple to go and I'm saving that for breaking point.

This has also been a very frustrating week concerning hotel services, for want of a better word. No matter how slowly and clearly we dictate our order to Room Service, we always seem to end up with somebody else's. I have developed an almost pathological addiction to their minestrone soup and strawberry ice cream and, as I've ordered it every day, sometimes twice, they've now managed to get it

right. But should we require anything else – like something for Grant to eat, for instance – it is asking the impossible. Hamburger and chips came up as a Russian salad, an omelette turned into a steak that I could have made a nice handbag out of, and two lightly boiled eggs arrived in the form of a bowl of chilli con carne that looked as if somebody had already eaten it. The last straw came when a simple order for toast and jam appeared as a waffle that would have been better employed mending a roof.

We have now decided to eat breakfast, at any rate, in the rather exotic-looking alfresco restaurant that has been highly recommended by various members of the production team. And we did so this morning, Sunday. It was indeed very pleasant and the food was good.

But as we tucked into our fresh fruit salad we became uncomfortably aware of what sounded like several waste disposal units working simultaneously somewhere to our rear. We were both desperate to look round when one of the units paused and we heard the words 'More bread here, Señor', accompanied by a blizzard of scrambled eggs, which passed just short of my right shoulder and landed on the floor next to me. The voice was unmistakably American and aggressively loud. I *had* to look round and, as I did so, the mouth opened again and the words 'Sweet rolls' came out with such force that the scrambled eggs the American was still in the process of masticating not only shot past my shoulder but this time ended up very nearly pebble-dashing a potted palm some twenty feet away.

They were like a family of Cabbage Patch dolls, grotesquely come to life and literally blown up out of all proportion. There was a man, a woman and a boy who was approximately nine years old, although age was difficult to determine as it had been almost completely obscured by obesity. The boy, who really did look as though someone had

taken a bicycle pump to his bottom and he was about to burst, turned to his mother and said, in a high-pitched whine and with a mouthful of scrambled egg, 'I want more Coke.' She in turn then lifted her huge wobbling arm and waved it at three gossiping waiters. She looked as if she'd been made out of yards of surgical rubber and a couple of tons of junket. We sat, fascinated, as skinny waiters scurried back and forth with orders of more bread rolls, Danish pastries and, finally, an ice cream for the child.

They eventually got up to leave, and I couldn't resist a last look round to see them in motion. The woman was bringing up the rear and, my God, was she! I've never seen anyone move in so many directions at the same time. As my old Dad would have put it, 'like five dogs fighting in a sack'.

We then finished our breakfast. Just as we were dealing with the bill, Grant said, 'Oh my God, don't look now but there's an even bigger, even uglier family just coming in.' I, of course, did look round – and, sure enough, there was a line of gigantic wobbling pink people, led by an enormous woman wearing a pair of minute shorts. How on earth had she got them on? It was just like one of those lateral-thinking puzzles involving large blocks of ice. Her legs appeared to be fused from mid-calf upwards.

They sat themselves down next to us like a family of amoebas and the humungous woman, another American, summoned the waiter by lifting one mammoth arm that looked like it should have an anchor tattooed on it. As she put her arm back down again, we were treated to a warm whiff of some unidentifiable perfume mixed unpleasantly with stale perspiration.

We left, and went for a very long walk on the beach. As the day went on we noticed more and more of these families of honey monsters wherever we went. We began to wonder whether there was a competition being held in Acapulco for the Fattest Family in the World, sponsored by a chocolate manufacturer, but then we realized that Acapulco was simply a popular holiday resort for a breed of American we'd never yet come across – the Midwesterner. The swimming pool was full of them – they all spoke with loud, piercing voices, their skins were either sickly white or badly burned red, they pulled out large wads of dollars whenever a waiter came near, and their conversation seemed to be solely concerned with what they had bought, what they were going to buy, what they had eaten and what they were going to eat. I've never seen so much cellulite in one place since we took my Auntie Kathleen on a day trip to Blackpool.

And GOLD – they were covered in it! Great ugly lumps of jewellery, gold blocks would have been more attractive or a bank statement made into a hat. One woman was so weighed down that when she dived in I was seriously worried for her safety, but she popped back up again like a rubber ball. Of course, with all her padding she's probably unsinkable. The funny thing is that, being eighteen weeks pregnant, I had been slightly embarrassed at the thought of sitting by the pool because of my shape. But I have to say that I had nothing to worry about because, looking round at the female bodies – and, come to think of it, the male ones, too – you'd be hard pressed to guess which one of us was pregnant!

___25 November 1987___

I'm in a bit of a way today. The hotel has lost my marvellous Mothercare support bra. It was wonderfully çomfortable with big wide straps – the sort big girls wore for hockey at school. It's the one garment a pregnant person simply mustn't be without. The midwife more or less warned me that even a day without it and I'd be capable of a new party trick – flipping

my lalas over my shoulders and tipping them back again with my heels. She even did a short but graphic mime to demonstrate. I was horrified. That bra has never left my body since. Well, not the same one, you understand, as I have two that I alternate – but now, of course, I only have one. The other one was replaced by a pair of small boy's Y-fronts. I tackled the laundry about it and they denied all knowledge of such a garment and said they'd be sending a man up to reclaim the Y-fronts. I said wouldn't that be a bit embarrassing for him? And, anyway, they were most certainly a boy's unless they'd been in a boil wash.

It has been one thing after another with the laundry. First of all it didn't come back at all for three days, and every time we rang to complain they said, 'Oh, do you want it?' as if it were something out of the ordinary to want your washing back. I'd been warned by various people on the set not to send anything that I valued, and it seemed like every day that someone would turn up with a newly acquired garment from the laundry. Some people did quite well – one bloke got a Gucci shirt instead of his wife's old nightie.

Finally we rang to complain again about the washing's non-appearance, whereupon we were told it had been delivered yesterday. Yes, it had, but to the wrong room. Eventually it reached us in the hands of a slimy little laundry person who asked, 'You 'ave a little something for me?' 'Oh, yes,' I replied, and handed him the Y-fronts.

He said, 'No, a little something', and obscenely rubbed his thumb and forefinger together like someone who'd just picked his nose.

'Pardon?' I said.

He dropped his obsequious smile and, with a harder tone, said, 'A tip.'

Grant pushed past me and picked the tiny man up under the arms so their faces were level with one another.

A huge blue vein sticking out of his neck, he said, *'I'll* give you a tip. Don't ask for fucking tips!' and threw him out into the corridor. Our balcony is now full of dripping clothes.

29 November 1987

The outstanding highlight of our three-week shoot in Mexico has got to have been yesterday's wrap party to mark the end of filming. It was held in this fabulous villa overlooking the bay. Actually it was the villa that was used in the film as Buster and June's home in Acapulco, and was where we did our last day's shooting.

The party was a totally spontaneous event which started almost the minute shooting stopped, when the producer was thrown, arms flailing and glasses flying, into the swimming pool. As the evening wore on everybody got the same treatment, apart from myself – I was exempt because of my condition, and I just sat regally at the side, watching the cavortings. This became most fun when, one by one, the freeloaders, hangers on and poseurs who are at every party connected with the showbusiness world, and all dressed to kill, were manhandled, with looks of absolute horror on their faces, into the pool.

One of them was a young man in a brilliant white suit and dark glasses (even though night had now fallen and we were outside), who was so cool he could hardly speak or move. He was like a constipated Mickey Rourke. The sight of him sailing through the air, face scarlet with rage and arms akimbo, gave me a lovely warm feeling inside.

This feeling was to recur later in the evening over two women who, during a brief conversation, had told me that they were loosely connected with someone who knew the film caterer's accountant, and had spent the entire evening searching with desperate eyes for a couple of men of influence and power.

They posed and minced around the pool wearing designer dresses and perfect make-up, but were clearly having difficulty in sorting out the important and mighty from the rest of us. Looking at the assembled sodden bunch, I could understand why. They sauntered up to several blokes, hoping they were a director or a producer, and actually missed the real director, who is anyway happily married and quite uninterested, and the real producer, who is a woman.

No, they approached the Mickey Rourke type, who was too busy trying to dry out his money (we found out later that he worked for a bank), one of the regular extras who was posing around, also in dark glasses, wearing tiny swimming trunks that looked as if they were concealing a small packet of fruit gums, and one of the actors' stand-ins who also looked like a cliché from the film world. In fact, the two women only really tried to pick up their male counterparts.

Eventually one of them came over to me and made small talk for approximately five seconds about what a fun evening it was, then abruptly asked if the director was here. I said, 'Oh yes, let me introduce you.' I mean, God forbid she should end up in bed with a boom operator!

I then took her over to Tony, a totally mad and massively randy Mexican, whose eyes lit up at the sight of her cleavage. Within seconds two hairy hands had given her breasts a jolly good squeeze, her bottom a slap, and had thrown her headlong into the pool. He then quickly followed so as to continue his harassment. I was apoplectic with laughter and her friend, seeing she'd pulled, asked me who he was. I said in reverential tones, 'The *director*.'

'Gosh, he looks quite fun,' she replied, and in she jumped. Tony cleans out the toilets in the actors' caravans.

We go home tomorrow.

5 December 1987

Just like Buster and June in the film, everyone couldn't wait to come home. I couldn't wait for a proper cup of tea and the luxury of making it myself. I couldn't wait to put my clothes in the washing machine and for them to come out still mine instead of being magically transformed into a strange child's underwear. I couldn't wait to sleep in my own bed – but above all I couldn't wait for the result of the amniocentesis.

I had avoided thinking about the subject because speculation about what we would do if there were any deformity in the foetus was unbearable. Mr P had said he would ring and leave a message on the answerphone if he needed to speak to us urgently. There was no message. This might be a good sign, but on the other hand maybe he had forgotten. Maybe he wanted to tell us to our faces. How could I get through the night and the next day?

I rang him as soon as possible today and he assured me everything was OK.

___15 December 1987___

I've been for my monthly check-up, at which Mr P asked me if I wanted to know the sex of the child, which the amnio had also revealed. Grant and I both most definitely wanted to know. I felt that refusing to know would have been like refusing to accept that the baby was a valid person until it was born. I thought it was ludicrous for a total stranger in a laboratory and a doctor who was no relation to know the sex of our offspring while we remained in ignorance. I also felt that privileged information such as this could only serve to improve my relationship with the little mite that was beginning its life in my womb, but many people we discussed the matter with were shocked that we should want to know. One man reacted with such outrage that you would think we had said we were going to boil the baby and then eat it, but in general people merely felt that it would spoil the wonderful surprise.

The surprise was wonderful anyway – it's going to be a girl. We're thrilled – but we would have been equally thrilled if it was going to be a boy, for the sex is not important in itself. What *is* really important is that the little bump that is now starting to show and to kick has lost its anonymity. It's not an 'it' anymore, it's a 'she'. We're going to call her Maisie – the name came from a copy of an old Victorian theatre poster in the back of a Dickens novel. We went through the motions of discussing other names and even bought a book of girls' names. Clea was discussed, and then we put it together with Roffey, Grant's surname – no, it's definitely going to be Maisie.

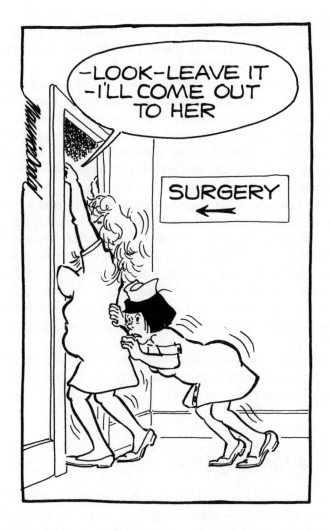

_____ 21 December 1987 _____

Our cleaner has just become a Jehovah's Witness. She announced this startling fact only this morning. I say 'startling' because Benita is an Italian Catholic and her grasp of the English language is slight, to say the least.

It happened, she claimed, a few weeks ago when a couple of Jehovah's Witnesses, neither of whom spoke Italian, came and knocked on her door. They left her with a huge leather-bound tome printed in English – her ability to read English I would rate at zero, because she ignores all the notes we leave for her, and her own are almost unintelligible ('A cup I crack, don't bless you with this – sorry!').

She talks about her conversion in a very off-hand way, as if it were one from electricity to gas, which makes me think she may well have misinterpreted what it is she has become caught up in, and now thinks she belongs to some club or that she is a representative of Freeman's Catalogues. However, I didn't want to become too involved for fear of her taking it into her head to convert me, so I steered the conversation towards my own obsession – MY CONDITION.

She then said her own daughter had been an enormous fourteen pounds at birth and had broken Benita's pelvis. I think I'd rather be converted!

_____ 4 January 1988 _____

The midwife came for the first of her prenatal visits today. She is marvellous – Joyce Grenfell in manner, positive, full of basic practical advice, and totally dismissive of negative thoughts and any old wives' tales such as if I were frightened by a horse during pregnancy, would the child be born with a mane down its back?

She opened heartily with 'Now your vagina is going to get very, very wet'. I regretted her saying this, as there was a man mending the washing machine in the kitchen, which was but feet from us.

Grant, however, murmured his appreciation. I can see foreplay going straight out of the window!

15 January 1988

G was calm as she felt the ache in the small of her back come and go. She had mastered the breathing techniques which had brought about vital relaxation. She felt that now, after months of concentrated yoga, relaxation was at her beck and call to be summoned at the very mention of the word 'contraction'. For the first time in her life, she knew what being relaxed really meant. She had prepared for the day, and now that day had come. There had been a little blood, she had been sick, but using her newly found knowledge she had achieved calm. She timed her contractions and even managed a light meal.

The contractions soon became very painful, but she steadily got her things together. Her nightie, some joss sticks, a collection of tapes of Indian sitar music and some fruit juice that she and her husband might sip during the forthcoming proceedings. Eventually the contractions were coming every five minutes and had become almost unbearable. It was time to leave. They bundled their belongings into the van after notifying the hospital they were on their way, with G exercising supreme control over the pain.

On arriving she could hardly resist a little smile in between contractions – a smile of total pleasure. Her first child would be born at any moment and she was handling it with practised serenity.

The midwife examined her and in a loud, matter-of-fact voice said, 'Well, you're so tense I can't even see your cervix, let alone see if it's dilated.'

She was put in a bath for two hours, after which it was then discovered that her cervix had dilated half an inch. She gave birth some twenty-four hours later with pain that made the aforementioned contractions seem like mild discomfort in comparison. Not a joss stick had been lit, not a note of Indian sitar music played – they were still in the van.

In fact the only sound to be heard, apart from that of human voices, was the ward clock, which had so jangled their nerves in the small hours that G's husband had ripped it from the wall.

G told me this story over lunch today. I joined her in her laughter as she remembered, and as we resumed our meal I found my appetite had quite disappeared.

___ 19 January 1988 ___

The midwife called again today to discuss my breasts, which are now of mammoth proportions. Men stare at them in the street, they sway in a matronly way and cause looks of awe and lust, and on one occasion I swear I spotted fear from a man with a moustache carrying a small handbag!

She said if I intended to breast-feed, which I did, I must start to express them every day.

I begged her pardon. Surely there was nothing in them yet?

She assured me there was and ordered me to show her my nipple, which I promptly did. Promptly, because I did not want to receive another stinging slap to the wrist which I got last week for going into hysterics at the sight of Grant in full squatting position doing the breathing exercises appropriate for labour. Not only that, but at her insistence he was also, with a very red face, staring me directly in the eye. This was, she said, so that he could give me complete support on the fateful day.

She then took my nipple between forefinger and thumb and squeezed with such force that it brought tears to my eyes. 'Sorry, darling,' she said. 'It might be better if you do it yourself.'

Grant, knowing full well the sensitivity of my nipples – having suffered in the past few weeks many a rebuff in the form of, 'Ow, that hurts, get off' – was looking on aghast, whereupon she turned on him and said, 'You could be helping with this.'

He blushed and said, 'No fear.'

21 January 1988

Well, the midwife was right. Every day after a couple of minutes' massage behind the nipple, little beads of colourless liquid – colostrum – have appeared. This practice apparently facilitates breast-feeding.

From the little chats and discussions that I have been involved with today at the local Baby Shop with assorted mums of varying experience, I gather breast-feeding can be anything from sheer ecstasy to absolute torture! One mum said it was so painful that she felt like throwing the baby out of the window! And when another, more earthy, type had commented that for her breast-feeding had been an almost sexual experience, the first woman retorted, 'Well, what are *you* into, whips and chains?'

A lady who was in the process of buying a pushchair for her new twin boys whilst her tiny daughter, unseen by her mother, shoved armfuls of babygros into her shopping bag, said the unpredictability of lactation was for her the biggest bane. The cry of any baby, didn't matter whose, would set her off a-leaking. This could happen anywhere, but favourite was Safeway's where she nearly always arrived at the checkout red-faced and flustered with twin maps of Ireland on her front for all the world to see. A tall Sloanish type with Fergie bow and pearls said that was nothing – the man next door's strimmer got her going!

Well, what I want is to breast-feed for as long as possible, a year being the limit. The thought of doing so any longer brings to mind a rather off-putting scene. It took place on the beach at Cannes. A little tot of about eighteen months was happily staggering about in the sand with his father. Suddenly with a shriek of delight he hurtled off in the direction of a nearby topless beauty whom he must have assumed to be his mother. He promptly fell on her and attached himself

limpet-like to her nipple. She too shrieked, but not with delight. The father then had the embarrassing task of extricating his son without molesting the woman!

__ 22 January 1988 _____

Today I went to an extremely trendy tea party in London's Docklands. It was at the home of a theatre director and his interior designer wife, and looked it, with a view over the Thames and Tower Bridge looming, enormous through the kitchen window. It was heaving with fashion-conscious luminaries and, to be perfectly frank, I felt uncomfortable.

I was just beginning to think of excuses to leave, like 'Oh, dear, I think I may have gone into labour', when an old actress pal entered the room. I was saved. She made a bee-line for me and we huddled together to dish the dirt. No sooner had she embarked on the juiciest bit of gossip I'd heard in ages – concerning an enormously rugged, macho and very famous film star who was leaving his wife for another man, who happened to be a not very good actor whom we both knew – when we were joined by a small mincing man wearing eye make-up and a rather lank ponytail. He plonked himself down with a bounce on to the coffee table in front of us. One skinny leg wrapped itself like bindweed around the other about seven times, an elbow landed on a knee and, in turn, a face landed on a waiting hand. Then, with a look of unspeakable boredom, the face said, 'Fuck him, and the horse he rode in on, dear.'

We both looked up to see to whom he was referring. It appeared to be a very handsome grinning black man wearing a stetson, cowboy boots and an open waistcoat which revealed that his nipples were pierced with a couple of gold sleepers. Given the tender condition of my own nipples, my eyes watered instantly. The mincing man offered no explanation for his outburst and then began, albeit with hushed tones, an uncalled for attack on our host, referring to him as 'she'.

'She couldn't direct piss into a bucket, dear. I wouldn't mind, but she couldn't direct the Mississippi past New Orleans, dear.'

He spat this tirade at us for about twenty minutes, by which time we, too, sported looks of unspeakable boredom. Then, as suddenly as he had arrived, he unravelled his legs, stood up and turned to rejoin his cowboy friend (and, presumably, his horse). As he did so, we noticed there was a piece of paper stuck to his back. Printed on it, in large letters, were the words 'I am a boring arsehole'.

My friend and I spontaneously exploded with laughter, as did the cowboy. Suddenly I felt a lovely warm sensation 'down below', which almost instantly became cold and wet. It was unthinkable. How could anything so devastatingly dreadful happen to me?

By now everyone had turned round to look in our direction because of our screeching laughter, and here I was on a cream-coloured sofa surrounded by gawping faces I didn't really know and I'd wet myself.

In seconds, with Girl Guide quick-thinking, I threw my Perrier over myself to mask whatever stain was fast appearing in my crotch and on the sofa. Through fits of laughter, and by now in a state of near-hysteria, I dug my friend in the ribs and said, 'Ooh, now look what you've made me do. I've spilled my drink.' Believing I'd now cónned everyone into thinking the damp patch was Perrier and not pee, I continued to enjoy the joke on the boring arsehole. But seconds later, with a quick glance down, I noticed that the large stain was steaming....

8 February 1988

Had another scan – baby now too big to see as a whole. Came away with a photo of her hand – it was so sweet! I kept getting it out and weeping over it until I suddenly noticed that it was the very same shape as Grant's, who is six feet tall and built like a brick powder room. He has since taken to calling her Mole. I stared blankly at him – he described an imaginary birth, with two huge hands tunnelling mole-like out into the world. I was not amused. The nickname has been dropped!

9 February 1988

I had to go to the hospital today for a special urine test, as my blood pressure looks dodgy. For this particular test a mid-stream specimen of urine is necessary. This entails cleansing yourself with a little mild disinfectant and catching some urine mid-stream. As I sat in the toilet with my little container for the urine and my disinfectant, I was reminded of an incident that took place during my days as a nurse.

I was on night duty, it was about midnight, and everyone was finally settled down. The ward was full but for one bed. That, too, would have been occupied but the man meant to be admitted that day hadn't shown up. Suddenly, as my colleague and I sat drinking our coffee at the night table, our attention was drawn to the sound of someone entering the ward. Coming through the gloom was the tottering shape of an old man. On spotting us he raised an arm in greeting and boomed, 'Hello, my darlings!' We shot towards him as bodies disturbed from sleep started to stir, and beds began to creak.

Amid lots of shushing, we asked him what he wanted.

At ear-splitting pitch, he explained that he was the admission that had failed to turn up. By this time bodies were sitting up, and requests for cups of tea were being made. Whilst my friend dealt with some of these, I ushered the aged patient to his bed, whisked the curtains around him and explained in hushed but urgent tones that it was imperative that he kept his voice down as people around him were trying to sleep.

He rounded on me in a voice even louder than before: 'Yes, yes, I know all that. There's no need to push.'

Threats on the old man's life were now coming thick and fast through the surrounding darkness.

'I'm deaf, you know,' he added.

It was a rule on this ward that all patients gave mid-stream specimens of urine before retiring on the day of admission. The thought of explaining all the ins and outs of such a procedure to this poor man, without waking the few remaining sleepers and whipping the others into a mutinous frenzy, was almost too much to contemplate. So I took him gently by the arm and guided him through the hostile darkness to the lavatory at the end of the ward. My task was not eased by the stone floor and tiled walls that caused even the most insignificant sounds to be echoed and amplified out into the ward.

However I began, with careful articulation, to explain that I wanted a specimen, and showed him the container in which he was to give it.

He looked bewildered, but obligingly nodded and said, 'I see.'

I then showed him the little pot of disinfectant and some cotton wool, and explained that he was to clean himself first.

He frowned, but said slowly, 'Yes.'

I went on to say how he was to pee into the toilet first,

then catch a drop and then finish off peeing into the toilet.

He was looking at me very suspiciously.

I said, 'Do you understand?' I was now talking as loudly as he was.

He answered 'Yes' in the way someone might if they were addressing a mad person who had said something totally outlandish, and then eased himself past me and scurried back to his bed.

Eventually, with some coaxing, I got him back to the toilet and decided I would get him started myself. So I soaked the cotton wool ball with disinfectant and went to undo his flies. As I got hold of his zipper he slapped my hand away and reeling backwards with a look of complete horror, he said in a shocked and offended voice of unbearable decibels, 'I'm old enough to be your father!'

I managed somehow to explain that my intentions were honourable. Finally he calmed down and seemed to understand, with much nodding, what was required of him. Now confident that he could be left to get on with it, I went to get on with more pressing duties.

A couple of hours later I popped into the toilet to collect the specimen. The container was there, but empty, and likewise the one containing the disinfectant. I went back to his bed but he was out cold, asleep.

Next morning when he woke I said, 'Er, Mr Newton, where is your specimen?'

He beamed, and in his storm-warning voice, said, 'Yes?'

'Your specimen?'

Irritated, he replied, 'Yes, yes, I drank the medicine!'

___11 February 1988___

My blood pressure is still up, and the baby is upside down! The doctor said she was sitting in my pelvis instead of her head being there. I thought it was extremely sensible of her to want to come out feet first, but he said it would mean a Caesarian. He then tried to move her himself. Without going into too much detail, it made me feel like a bizarre glove puppet! She refused to budge. That's my daughter!

___22 February 1988___

Today is my thirty-eighth birthday. Of course, this now has a new significance. I find myself constantly referring to my mother's description of my birth which, all told, seems to have been pretty awful. The details of it are firmly imprinted on my memory. Not that I remember the event itself, but my mother has given me a fairly graphic description whenever the subject of childbirth – no matter what the context – has been brought up. I can still hear her voice floating clearly up the stairs when, on my fifteenth birthday, I was made a captive audience thanks to a bout of flu which had confined me to bed.

'Fifteen years ago today,' the Irish brogue, dramatic in its rendering, began, 'I woke at 6 a.m. and knew I was in trouble.'

'Why?' I croaked back.

'Because I was passing your motions,' she said, her voice lowered to convey the gravity of this last statement. (For years this had me mystified, and whenever I questioned my mother as to its meaning she simply repeated it in an extremely irritated fashion: 'I WAS PASSING YOUR

MOTIONS', as if that were an explanation in itself.)

The voice continued, 'I had Asian flu. Your father and I got straight on the bus.'

On the bus! It's unimaginable! The story then picks up at the hospital.

'They gave me a big fish dinner. After me warning them you were on the way! Of course, I was sick all over the bed. A temperature of 105 degrees and the cord was around your neck. You were in distress.' (I should think I was!) 'They had to call in the priest and your father was asked to choose between you and me.'

And with that she swept back into the kitchen to resume whatever it was she had been doing. I'd never heard this last detail before about 'the decision', which clearly in the end did not have to be made. But my father *was* asked, so a couple of years later I plucked up the courage to quiz him about it.

'Well, I had to choose your mother,' he said. 'Imagine how she'd have felt if I'd chosen you.'

___16 March 1988___

Grant has just come home with the groceries. These included several bean salads. I thought this was rather brave, considering the wind situation.

This as yet unmentioned problem started at about eighteen weeks when I'd finished filming *Buster*. It also coincided with my being put on iron tablets. It seems to be particularly treacherous at night. I daren't sleep with my back to Grant for fear of finding him comatose in the morning, so I tend to sleep with the windows open and my bottom poking out of the duvet. With this method, the offensive gases are let out

into the air as opposed to being trapped under the duvet. If trapped, any movement by the sleepers can cause the gas to leak out, possibly into the pillow area.

This oughtn't to be of huge concern, except that, thinking back over the weeks, there were some mornings when Grant was extremely difficult to waken. If the gases are allowed freely into the room by the exposed bottom method they seem to hover in deadly pockets, to be blundered into by unsuspecting persons on their fourteenth visit to the toilet. Now as this person is generally me, at four or five in the morning, I think it's the fairest way of dealing with this only too common problem, which can be particularly bothersome in enclosed spaces – for example in a lift, or in the company of other people. If the problem should occur in such places, I would advise looking pointedly at someone else.

_____ *24 March 1988* _____

Bills are flooding in at a frightening rate of knots from the hospital for scans and blood tests as every small question mark in my and my family's medical history is put under a microscope. My grandmother was a diabetic so today I've been given a sickening amount of glucose to drink, followed by a nurse taking six blood samples at half-hourly intervals. I now have to keep my right arm covered in case people think I'm a drug addict.

___26 March 1988_____

It's my best friend's birthday party, so I went to look for party gear. I told the assistant that I wanted something flattering to my shape. Thinking she would understand, I went browsing through the rack, only to hear her snorting to her mates, 'The fat one in the big brown sweater.' My face burned into a blush, my eyes filled with tears and I left unable to speak. What on earth is up? A few months ago I would have told her to stick her garments where the sun doesn't shine.

___6 April 1988_____

Yesterday, at my weekly check-up, I was greeted by the marvellous news that my glucose tolerance test was abnormal and that my blood pressure is about to be dangerous. So I'm getting a foretaste of the Portland – I was admitted last night. It's like a five-star hotel, only twice as expensive. I'm in mainly to rest so that my blood pressure hopefully goes back down but also to have my blood sugar checked properly. For the latter, I am under a man called Mr De Sweet. Yes, really!

Part of the investigation involves me having to test my own blood sugar level, before and after meals. This was demonstrated for me by a rather nervous, diminutive Irish midwife who looked for all the world like Olive Oil and spoke with the same speed and urgency as someone commentating on the last fifty yards of the Grand National. 'First you have to prick your finger and make it bleed,' she almost ordered, and then, obviously sensing that I wasn't too keen, volunteered to prick her own finger to show that no pain need be involved. She must have stood there for a full minute, holding the tiny pin in a rather shaky hand and staring very hard at her thumb as if the staring itself might draw blood, like a karate expert about to smash a brick with one hand. And then, with about the same force as would be used for the above, she stabbed the pin into her thumb, at the same time letting out an almighty shriek. There was blood everywhere – the bedspread, her uniform, my nightie. I was beginning to think she might need stitches. Then, grabbing a bunch of tissues and clasping them to her thumb, she looked at me and said, quite calmly, as if her little demonstration had gone perfectly, 'OK?'

The next step in this procedure is to catch a drop of blood on the end of a little perspex strip called a BM stick. Whatever colour this goes, after about a minute, will indicate the amount of sugar in your blood. I had seen this procedure before when I was a nurse and knew that there was really nothing to it, and, after the midwife's rather cowardly and inept attempt, I couldn't wait to show her what I was made of and get it over with.

Impatiently I grabbed one of the pins and, in a manner of speaking, positioned myself for the prick. A couple of minutes later I too was staring at my thumb, my other hand shaking somewhere nearby. I simply couldn't bring myself to do it. It took several attempts, the first few with my eyes shut. I stabbed my leg, my stomach and my hand. Eventually I did it. That was twenty-four hours ago. I still find it hard and I'm running out of fingers.

9 April 1988

My blood pressure is now almost totally normal. The night sister popped in to tell me that the actress Linda Bellingham – the mum in the Oxo ad – was in the upstairs ward having just had her son a couple of days ago. She has been asking if she could pop down and see me – we share the same agent. I agreed, of course. She has had a Caesarian and her husband, an Italian restaurateur, was present throughout the birth. She said that some time after the event, when they were alone, he whispered urgently, 'Linda, I must tell you... I saw your liver. I know I did. I recognize it from the restaurant.'

12 April 1988

Mr P has told me that the baby will more than likely be delivered two weeks today. My God, the nursery still looks little more than a store room! I spoke to Grant, and he suggested we paper it with bills from the hospital. I thought it was rather tasteless and said as much. The hospital bills are blue.

17 April 1988

It seems I've got gestational diabetes, which only occurs during pregnancy. It is the same as ordinary diabetes, and just as unglamorous. Anyway, I am now on a sugar-free diabetic diet. This is served by several laughing oriental girls whose grasp of English is minimal, to say the least, and who have, quite obviously, never heard the word 'diabetic'. When I complained that they had put sugar on the grapefruit they found it hilarious, so I resorted to repeating 'NO sugar', very loudly, several times in succession. They then stopped and stared at me. 'I am a diabetic,' I explained.

'D...iet,' one of them said slowly, like a baby uttering the word for the first time.

'Yes,' I enthused.

'Yes,' she repeated happily. 'You fat.'

This is how I am now greeted every time they bring in a meal – 'You fat' with lots of pointing and giggling. Just now one of them brought in a cup of tea. I waited for the customary 'You fat', but it did not come. Instead, she looked at me steadily and asked, 'Where is your baby?'

'In here,' I said, pointing at my stomach. With a look of horror, she left. She obviously thinks I've eaten it.

Is there no escaping pneumatic drills in London? There's one constantly serenading me on a nearby roof, there's one near the back of our house, accompanied by a power driver, and there's one in the road in front of our house. This baby probably won't be able to sleep without one!

21 April 1988

A man in a green gown, wearing a J-cloth on his head, came in to take blood. He said he was very excited at meeting me. I was flattered until he responded to a little joke I made with 'Oh, Tracy, you are funny.' I, of course, put him straight, much to his embarrassment. 'Oh yes,' he said, 'you work with that other girl. Marvellous!'

The 'other girl' – that is, Victoria Wood – came to visit me this afternoon, during which time the young leech returned for more blood. On seeing us both, he said, 'Oh, I've got you both here!' and went out humming the theme tune to *French and Saunders*. I am deeply depressed.

___ *22 April 1988* ___

I dreamt my fridge was full of Mars bars. I woke up with the taste of one faithfully reproduced on my tongue – BLISS. Then I tucked into my sugar-free breakfast of Weetabix and half a grapefruit. My salivary glands shrank in disappointment at the sight of it.

___ *25 April 1988* ___

It's impossible to get my mind round the fact that in the morning, with absolutely no preparation (by which I mean labour and birth), I will, at approximately 8.10, be presented with a tiny person. I talked to her, 'her' being Maisie, at length in the bath this evening to try to prepare her for what I imagine must come as a bit of a shock. I mean how would you feel, dear reader, if one morning, quite unexpectedly whilst you were partaking of a little amniotic fluid, your warm and rosy horizons were rent asunder and two gigantic hands yanked you out into the cold light of an alien world? Answer me that.

26 April 1988

I tried to sleep, but without success. Images of mammoth babies distorted out of all proportion by diabetes filled my mind's eye, alternating with scrawny little scraps of life deprived of nutrition due to my high blood pressure. I decided to read and got out my wonderful Patricia Highsmith short stories – what do I pick? One about a couple with a Down's syndrome baby! Although the amnio had reported that the foetus was normal, what was chilling was that there was a paragraph describing how unusually quiet the baby was while in the womb. This made my heart stop, as Maisie has been electronically monitored for foetal movement and heartbeat every day this week and, since I've been in hospital, every four hours. And they're forever making well-meaning comments like 'Ooh, a little bit quiet. Perhaps she's asleep. I think we'd just better do another reading.' I'm sick to bloody death of the sight of this monitor.

Eventually, mind racing, fully convinced that my baby couldn't possibly be born normal, I rang for the midwife and agreed to take the sleeping pill they'd offered me earlier, for, as she quite rightly pointed out, it would be the last good night's sleep I'd be getting for some time.

During the night I woke with a jolt, having dreamt that my period had started while sleeping on Sir Peter Hall's sofa. I've only met Sir Peter briefly a couple of times and have never sat, let alone slept, on his sofa. As for having a period on it – well, it's unthinkable!

Anyway, gradually becoming aware of my surroundings, and feeling rather damp down below, I reached out and turned on the overhead light. I had wet myself, or so it seemed. I eased myself off the bed and lumbered into the bathroom. There was water dripping down my legs on to the floor. I couldn't believe my waters had broken – it was too much of a coincidence. To come in for an elected Caesarian and then for my waters to break the night before! So I sat on the bed for another couple of hours, not wanting to bother anyone and unable to sleep while water was trickling out periodically into a bundle of tissues.

At 4 a.m. it started to flow out more rapidly, and the slight backache I'd been experiencing turned into an almost unbearable pain which I then timed. It was every twenty minutes. This must be it, I thought, and rang for the midwife.

She got out the dreaded monitor and strapped me to it, saying there was nothing to worry about. But the pain worsened, so I called her back, thinking each contraction was so violent that I must be about to give birth. She simply smiled and turned the monitor round so I could see the reading for contractions. The machine looks like a lie detector, with a needle tracing on paper any movement the womb makes. Well, had it been a lie detector I would be Miss Honesty 1988, for I could see nothing except, every so often, a minute hiccup in an otherwise straight line.

Clutching my back, I asked, 'Is this thing accurate?' 'Ooh yes,' she said and then added ominously, 'This is only the beginning.' She then pointed out the extent the needle would move if I were in rip-roaring labour. I was astonished – it meant I was only feeling about a tenth of the pain I'd be experiencing at the height of labour. Thank God for the epidural I was going to have!

According to the midwife, it's quite common for women knowing they're about to have a Caesarian to go into labour, and I have to say I was thrilled. I felt that Maisie and I really *had* had a chat in the bath and that we were in tune with one another and had synchronized our watches for the forthcoming event. I felt great pleasure and excitement at each contraction, and couldn't wait for Grant to arrive so that I could announce that Maisie would have been born today anyway, and that we weren't dragging her untimely from her mother's womb, as Shakespeare sort of put it.

Grant came at 6.30, looking as if he'd already given birth at least twice, with a big pale face, dark stains under his eyes and hair endearingly sticking up like Stan Laurel. I told him the good news, the tired face lit up with emotion and we hugged each other as best we could, with the monitor and my bulk not helping, and then we sat holding hands in the dimly lit little room, saying nothing for there was nothing more to say.

At seven we were taken down to the theatre ante-room, the drip and epidural were inserted with no discomfort, and I felt on top of the world. I looked round to find Grant, who loathes hospitals, looking as though he was about to give birth a third time. He was taken out in a very wobbly condition for a cup of tea!

At eight we were taken into a very pleasant and bright theatre, and Mr P came in in a jolly and businesslike mood. Grant sat to the right of my head and we chatted hysterically as they inserted the catheter and started the op.

It was the most extraordinary experience. I felt absolutely nothing from the waist down, except a little pulling and tugging, but no pain. Mr P accompanied the proceedings with a running commentary. 'Here she comes, here she comes, here's her bottom. Oh, she looks just like her mother, she's as bald as a coot.'

It was as if Grant and I were watching someone else give birth. Then, just five minutes after the op had started, there was a little reedy cry and a beautiful pink baby, who didn't look like anybody, was lifted up over the screen that concealed the actual operation. I said, 'Hello, who are you?' She was handed to Mr Mac, the paediatrician, for a quick check, then wrapped in a J-cloth and put on my chest. Immediately she stopped crying and I started. She stared

intently at me, and when Grant spoke she stared at him in the same way, ignoring all other voices in the room. She smelt divine – I wanted to lick her all over.

They were going to take her and wash her but I said, 'Ooh no, don't. Please don't bother. Don't bother to wrap her, I'll take her just as she is.' I could feel emotion surging up inside me as Grant then took her and held her. My throat went into a tight spasm and my eyes filled. 'No,' I thought. I couldn't let the lid off this bubbling pot of emotion until I was in the privacy of my own room. I succeeded in keeping it down by cracking a joke that I don't remember, and when the stitching was finally finished, some forty minutes later, we were wheeled out to the lift.

By now my throat was aching and dry and I couldn't speak, paralysed by the weight of feeling that urgently needed release. Someone said something about the lift having broken down, so we ended up in a very tight squeeze in the service lift, which smelt of cabbage and was badly in need of a drop of paint. It was such an unfitting exit to the most spectacular scene of my life that the tonnage of emotion waiting just behind my tonsils was simultaneously released and transformed into torrents of wonderful relief-giving laughter.

When we arrived back in the ward Maisie was taken off to the nursery for some blood tests, just to make sure the diabetes had had no effect. Then, drunk on elation and whatever it is they put in the epidural, I rang my mother and had a long conversation, not a single detail of which can I remember. I then lay drumming my fingers on the counterpane, waiting for our little darling to be restored to us. It had been twenty minutes. It was too much, we couldn't wait any longer.

Grant, by now rather agitated, jumped up and said, 'This isn't right. Where is she? She should be with us. I'm going to get her!'

He then rushed from the room and seconds later was in the nursery, where he pointed directly at some poor woman who was learning to bath a very new baby and accusingly said, somewhat hysterically. 'You've got my child!'

Terror-struck, she looked at her infant and then back at Grant and, in a hurt and rather defensive voice, said, 'No, I haven't.'

He then wildly scoured the nursery and, on locating our tiny bundle, proceeded to wheel her out, muttering apologies to the woman. A nursery nurse then blocked his path, saying, 'Wait a minute, we haven't done her blood test.'

'Why not? She should be with her mother,' fumed Grant.

'Well, we're very busy,' said the nurse.

'Well, we're not,' replied Grant and stormed back to the room, bringing Maisie with him.

What followed is a wonderful hazy blur, dominated by a single image – a tiny, perfect face with a cupid's bow for a mouth and a smattering of spun gold for hair. We thought her entirely beautiful. I spoke to my sister-in-law and she said that when her first child was born she was convinced that the other mothers in the ward were consumed with envy whenever they saw him, and consequently filled with disappointment when they saw their own babies. And she actually felt sorry for them. We, too, pitied several sets of parents on seeing some of their offspring, and Grant was forever coming back from the nursery saying, 'Oh my God, you should see Mrs So-and-so's twins, they're horrific. She must find it really difficult to feed them!'

27 April 1988

Because of the many tubes emanating from my body, namely the drip, the catheter, the drain for the wound and the soon-to-be-removed epidural, I hadn't had a good night. It wasn't so much a night's sleep as a series of uncomfortable dozes. I was woken from one of these in the early morning by a nursery nurse bringing in Maisie all swathed in pink, fast asleep in what looked like a fish tank on wheels. She left her by my bed and I dozed off again whilst staring lovingly at the tiny head.

A little later I awoke to the sound of her hunger cries. I went to press the bell for assistance and found it was not in its usual place tucked under my pillow but had fallen away out of reach. I tried to get at it but couldn't because I was so completely incapacitated, so I started to shout for the midwife. At this the baby's cries, which were already pretty urgent, rose to a desperate pitch. Nobody came. I didn't dare shout any more as I felt it was distressing the baby. I looked at her bright red face, its little features distorted by anger and frustration at not being fed. I was utterly helpless. My heart started to race and sweat popped up in a thin film all over my face. This was awful. Panic rose in me like milk in a saucepan.

Then I noticed the phone. It was about twenty-five miles away on the bedside locker, but nearer than the bell. With superhuman effort I managed with one hand to pull it towards me by the cord, the other hand clutching my wound. After knocking just about everything off my locker, I eventually had it in my grasp. Frantically I dialled the switchboard, the baby now apoplectic with rage and panic.

'Portland Hospital,' the friendly lilting voice announced.

'Yes, I know,' I said through gritted teeth. 'Please put me through to the second floor.'

'To whom do you wish to speak?' the sing-song voice asked.

'Anyone,' I said, barely disguising my irritation. 'A midwife, a nursery nurse, the cleaner!' I screamed.

There was a short silence on the other end. 'The cleaner? In connection with what?'

I was speechless with frustration. Everything this woman said was in the same speech pattern. It was like talking to an answerphone. 'Just put me through to the second floor,' I said in as controlled a voice as I possibly could.

'May I ask who is calling?' she sang.

'Julie Walters,' I spat.

'You wish to speak to Julie Walt...'

'I *am* Julie Walters.'

There was a long silence. 'Oh, you're ringing from your room?' a very small voice said.

'No, a local nightspot. I have been raving it up all night and now I would like to come back and feed my baby. Could you send a taxi?' I was connected to the second floor without further ado, and almost before I put the phone down an apologetic midwife bustled in and rushed round to Maisie. We both stared into the tank. She was asleep.

A couple of hours later a lovely African midwife came in and asked happily, 'Now, would you like to get up and have a little bath?' I thought this was a joke and laughed appropriately.

'We will remove your drip and catheter first,' she added, and did so with lightning efficiency. She wasn't joking, and the next five minutes or so I wouldn't particularly like to repeat. However, she was brilliant and kind and knew exactly how to get me moving, but all the way through the manoeuvre I had visions of my wound bursting open and the metal clips that were holding it together being shot out one by one and embedding themselves cartoon-like in the bathroom door. After much wincing, puffing and clutching of abdomen, I reached a sort of standing position and then proceeded very slowly to shuffle to the toilet, the midwife in my wake carrying the drainage bottle. It was a great feeling, I was free. Only one tube left but I could move, albeit it like an ancient Mrs Overall. This morning's incidents could never happen again.

30 April 1988

I was warned by several people about this day – the day my breasts filled with milk. The warning was that I would most likely become very emotional and I would not be able to stop crying.

Well, the milk started to come in yesterday, and I thought, 'What? I feel superb! Nothing could possibly bring me down. It's only neurotic women who let their hormones get the better of them who end up blubbering wrecks.'

This morning I woke up with breasts that could force Chesty Morgan into retirement. They were huge, hard and hot. My nipples, from which my little angel has drawn blood whilst breast-feeding, are now bruised and very painful, and on the advice of the midwife in charge I've been sitting with my back to the door and breasts exposed to the air to help heal the ailing nips.

A pile of post had arrived and, generally feeling I'd escaped the weeping and wailing and congratulating myself on coming through this potentially upsetting time pretty unscathed, I opened the first envelope. It was from two people I haven't seen for a couple of years and to whom I've never been particularly close. The card carried a simple message: 'Congratulations.' I wept buckets. I haven't been so moved since _Bambi_.

I sobbed continuously for two hours. At the same time milk started to pour from each breast, and this appears to be prompted by the phone ringing. Every time it rings they are filled with an extraordinary sensation that borders on both orgasm and pain, and then milk issues forth quite copiously.

When Grant arrives for his daily visit there is a very pathetic little creature waiting to greet him. My clothes sodden, my hair stuck down around a painfully red and swollen face, I managed between gulps and sobs to utter, 'Oh, Grant, I'm so happy!'

___2 May 1988___

The thought of leaving the security and expertise of the Portland, where highly qualified staff were on call at all times, was daunting – so much so that I felt compelled to pop a few souvenirs into my bag. I was busy doing this when Grant arrived to collect us. He watched for a while as I tried to squash a couple of pink baby blankets with 'Portland Hospital' emblazoned all over them into my already bulging bag. Then he laid a restraining hand over them and said, 'I think we should ask if we can buy a blanket.'

I was appalled. 'After paying £300 a night we should be able to take the bed,' I said. But he was right. Instantly I had an image of newspapers coming off the presses, like you see in old films, with vast headlines reading: 'Actress in hospital theft drama'. 'Actress left our cupboards bare,' says Portland midwife. I began to unpack.

Grant's eyes took on a fixed stare of astonishment as I emptied the loot on the bed – a couple of baby wraps, a couple of baby nighties, a towel, another pink blanket, powder and cream for Maisie's bottom, cotton wool, a few nappies and several pairs of disposable knickers. 'I've got just two words to say to you,' he said. 'Isobel Barnet.'

I did a quick mime, meaning 'Fair enough', scooped Maisie out of her fish tank and off we went. Grant installed us in the back of the old Daimler, with Tina Turner for accompaniment as we drove home.

I was unprepared for what followed. The contrast between the warm, rarefied, womb-like atmosphere of the hospital and the abrasive, loud, aggressive London we were now surrounded by was just too great, as I looked at this brand-new vulnerable bundle of complete innocence dressed in the teeniest babygrow we could find – the legs of which still hung a good six inches below her feet and the arms of which were folded back into big thick cuffs around her chubby wrists. She was so clean, new and trusting and the world outside was so big, dirty and dangerous – I shook with sobs all the way home, my already surging emotions fuelled with lyrics like 'Some people got to stay together', 'Love one another', 'Save it for a rainy day'. . . . Oh, my god, I caught sight of myself in the mirror as we turned into St Dionis Road, and with my swollen eyes and puffy face I looked as if *I'd* just come through the birth canal – never mind the baby.

A major miracle then occurred. We found a parking space only a hundred yards from our front door!

It was Benita's day to clean, so Grant went in to check that she had left as we both felt this was one time that we should be on our own together with Maisie. He had dropped huge hints like, 'Please be finished by midday.' It was now 1.30, but by the look on his face as he strode back to the car I knew she was still there. We drove round the block a couple of times and picked up a cup of tea from a greasy spoon. We returned a second time. Still she hadn't left. It was now two o'clock.

'She's dusting biros,' Grant said furiously. 'She's clearly hanging on to see the baby.' Now dying to go to the lavatory and tired of hiding my big red swollen face from the neighbours, I decided to give in. Grant heaved us both out of the car and, livid, we entered the house.

Sure enough there was Benita, busy arranging the telephone directories in alphabetical order, a task which judging by the puzzled expression on her face was giving her some trouble. Benita is rather a depressing person. She has a set face, a monotonous voice and a tendency to find the negative side to every situation. The conversation went as follows.

'Let me see baby. Oh, she's very small. Premature eh?'

'No,' I said. 'No, she's six pounds.'

Benita: 'Oh, she look very small. My daughter was fourteen pounds.'

I couldn't bare a repeat of the broken pelvis story in my sensitive condition so I cut in acidly, 'Oh, yes. Oh, dear. Oh, dear me, yes, very overweight. Maisie's just right.'

Benita: 'She sleep?'

'Oh yes, she's been wonderful.'

Benita: 'Hah, let's hope it last. Oh, what I had, my daughter, she sleep in hospital and then... she no sleep.'

She then put on her coat, at the same time managing to sweep a vase off the kitchen table, smashing it on the floor. Maisie's eyes flickered but she did not wake. Benita apologised by means of an 'Oh, crikey' and started to sweep it up into a metal dustpan. The resulting clatter caused Maisie's eyes to flicker again, but still she did not wake. Eventually Benita left with the parting line, 'My daughter, two years she no sleep.' With that she banged the front door so loudly I thought the front window was going to come out. Maisie's eyes shot open, her bottom lip loomed up in protest to cover her top one and she let out one hell of a wail. Poor Benita – what bad luck her daughter did not sleep for two years.

8 May 1988

This week has been pervaded by an unreal, almost dreamlike quality, probably because of the newness of our situation and the fact of being up all night. It's been like a mixture of Christmas and some unknown crisis. When I said this to Grant he said he saw no difference between Christmas and a crisis.

My emotions have continued to surge and dive uncontrolled. I simply dare not watch the news any more. A piece on the goings on in the Gaza Strip had me racked for hours the other night and left me empty and low for some time. It seems my new-found sensitivity and depth of awareness isn't confined to world affairs, for an innocuous *Tom and Jerry* cartoon reduced me to a Niagara of tears over Tom's cruelty.

I think what I have been experiencing is my maternal instinct. One morning I came down to find the cat had left a

baby bird dead on the kitchen floor. It hardly had feathers, it was so young, and looking at the back of its vulnerable bald little head my heart swelled with emotion at the loss of its innocent life. For a brief second it was Maisie's head, it was her life. It is as if, whenever I see anything or anyone that is in any way innocent or vulnerable, I am consumed by an overwhelming desire to protect.

Anything from a tiny puppy to a full-grown man can spark off these feelings. A couple of days ago we went out, for the first time since Maisie's birth, to see *Wall Street* at a local cinema. One of its stars, Charlie Sheen – who must be all of twenty-five and probably more – had this very effect on me. I felt painfully loving and desperately protective towards him. To all intents and purposes he *was* Maisie, at least for the duration of the film. As far as I was concerned he even looked like Maisie, yet he must be getting on for six feet tall, dark, slim and a man. She's about seventeen inches, fair, chubby, bald and a girl. I am quite clearly going doolally.

13 May 1988

Maisie now sleeps in her own room next door to us. She has done so since about the fourth day home. Sleep was impossible for either of us with her in the same room. On the first night when she cried for the first time we both simultaneously leapt from our respective sides of the bed and met with a painful clashing of foreheads at the side of her cot, almost knocking one another out. We only did that once, as Grant is pretty redundant at nocturnal feeding times. However, every tiny snort and murmur made our bodies go rigid, so next door she went.

22 May 1988

The old nipples, which I had been assured would heal and harden in just a week or so, were more painful than ever. The sight of that pretty little cupid's bow making its way towards one of them brought me out in a cold sweat. I finally reached breaking point when Maisie was about three weeks old. Totally exhausted from lack of sleep, trying to recuperate from a major abdominal operation and a particularly painful feed caused me to collapse in tears.

Grant said right, that was it, plucked Maisie from me, stuck her in the Snugglie and left. I sat forlornly on the sofa feeling hopeless and sorry for myself.

Ten minutes hadn't passed when he was back with a device that looked like it was meant for icing cakes. I thought, 'Oh, no, his sweet tooth has got the better of him again. This is wholly inappropriate' – and I told him so. He then brought the apparatus over and it turned out to be a breast pump. It was to be the saving of me. Grant could help out in the night and the nips would get a break.

The little hand pump, not greatly efficient, was replaced in a couple of days by an electric pump hired from the National Childbirth Trust, and this was sheer bliss. Not only was it easy – all I had to do was switch it on and sit there – but it was also extremely pleasant. In fact I whipped off a letter of recommendation to _Forum_ after only one session.

My milk supply must have trebled in the first week of use,

and the bedroom where we kept and used the pump looked like a bottling plant. Grant made a small sign which read 'Express Dairies' and stuck it on the fridge door – for it was full, as was the freezer. My mother, never one for waste, suggested I made a couple of rice puddings. She was serious.

3 June 1988

In four days' time Maisie will be six weeks old and, according to an official note we received a week or so back, if we don't register her birth within the next forty-eight hours someone will be round to see us. So today we walked down to Fulham Town Hall with Maisie strapped to Grant's chest by means of the Snugglie, her cosiness made complete by Grant's huge overcoat enclosed around her.

On arrival in the dark Victorian building, smelling of bureaucracy and disinfectant, we followed a faded little arrow which read 'Registry of Births and Deaths' and eventually found ourselves in a tiny waiting room. It contained several canvas and metal tubular chairs surrounding what looked like a school table with five or six ancient and tattered magazines scattered on it. The room had a frosted window which allowed in very little light, and sitting there in the gloom were four people who, judging from their faces, could only have been there to register deaths.

We sat ourselves down in a corner, opposite a couple of about sixty who looked pale, drawn and depressed. To our left was a woman in her late forties and next to her was a thin, mid-thirtyish man who looked so unwell I wondered if he had come to register his own death. Our arrival had obviously interrupted a conversation which had been taking place between the woman and the couple, and after we sat down, with a couple of minutes' grace, it was resumed. The man in his sixties spoke in tones so hushed they were almost inaudible. It was as if with every word he spoke he feared the building would fall down.

'Didn't she have any family?' he asked.

The late fortyish woman, who turned out to be Irish and not at all worried about the safety of the building, replied: 'No bugger came near.' The statement like a headline.

'Oh... dear,' the man and woman said, almost in unison. With this, Maisie let out one of her sweet little sighs, 'Haaa.'

The Irish woman immediately turned to me and said, 'Yeah, bloody terrible, isn't it?' She, clearly thinking it was me that had sighed – Maisie being totally hidden inside Grant's coat.

'What did she die of?' the old man continued.

'Oh, nothing serious,' came the reply.

Just then the door to the waiting room burst open and in bounced a young man, a vision of pastel from waist to neck, wearing a pair of bright red spectacles and to top it all a very tight perm. He would have looked more fitting trying to sell you a £200,000 garage in Chiswick than registering the death of your Great Aunt Deirdre.

He quickly ushered the Irish woman through another door into his office, and almost immediately our dim little room was lit up by the depressing glow of several fluorescent lights shining through a partly glazed partition. No one spoke. The silence was then broken by some muffled sobs coming from the office, accompanied by some comforting mutterings from the estate agent. Then silence again.

Another couple came in, one of them wearing a black armband and both of them looking extremely glum. Another half an hour must have passed, with us all desperately avoiding eye contact with one another and pretending not to hear the occasional sobs penetrating the partition. Just as the stillness and the silence seemed at their most oppressive, from the sleeping bundle in the depths of Grant's overcoat came what sounded like the noise of a tiny engine spluttering into life. It was a fart, and probably the longest and most musical in the history of mankind.

Grant reddened as looks of disgust hit him from all directions. Maisie invisible, to the assembled audience he was clearly the culprit. The fart seemed to go on for ever. Whole seconds passed as it reached its crescendo and then fut-fut-futted into silence. The looks of disgust turned to outrage. How could this young man be so disrespectful when they were there to register the death of their loved ones? How could he sit there and break wind... *and* whilst reading the *Listener*?

With the speed of light I ripped Grant's coat open to reveal a sleeping Maisie for all to see. Relief melted over their faces, quickly turning into smiles all round except for the couple with the armband, who did not smile at all.

Eventually we were called in by the estate agent and, as we stood up to make our way across the room, a small wet explosion hit the air again from the depths of Grant's overcoat. The couple with the armband, now the only ones left, just sat staring grim and stony-faced and the woman said, 'My, we have got wind, haven't we?'

Grant said, 'We certainly have', and another explosion followed in quick succession. This time there could be no confusion about its resonance and volume; it was quite obvious from whose bottom it had issued forth. He smiled wickedly at the couple and in we went.

MARRIAGE

If, dear reader, you were to ask me what is the question I have been asked more times than any other, I think in third place would be 'Are you who I think you are?', running a close second would be 'Would you like a cup of tea?' and definitely first would be 'What was it like to work with Michael Caine?' Well, these have all now been knocked clean out of the running by 'Are you going to get married now?' – 'now' referring to the fact that my position has changed due to my motherhood and hinting that getting married shows an intention on my part to become a responsible adult.

I have to say I have never been particularly enamoured by the thought of marriage, even in my early teens when all my contemporaries dreamt of and aspired to the engagement ring and then Naming the Day. I saw it as the shutting of a rather important door, namely my youth, which I felt should last as long as my life. Youth to me was summed up not in years but by an attitude which to me seemed incompatible with what I'd seen of marriage.

When I was seventeen I had a temporary job in an office in Birmingham. I was one of two juniors – the other was a girl called Lynn, who was fifteen. She was a big girl full of good fun, with a voice like a foghorn, and her one and only ambition was to be married. She was simply passing time until that wonderful day arrived. She asked me how old I was. 'Seventeen,' I replied.

'Am you engaged?' she asked, her Black Country voice full of concern.

'No,' I replied.

'Blimey!' she said, the word reverberating deafeningly around the office toilet. 'If I'm not engaged by the time I'm seventeen, I'll cut me wrists.'

I saw Lynn three years later up Smethwick High Street. She was pushing a pram with a very tiny baby in it and a toddler of somewhere between a year and eighteen months sitting on the pram grizzling. She had a huge black eye, her face had hardened and she looked utterly run-down. I count this as one of the saddest pictures I have ever seen in my life. The fun, the dreams, the hope and the youth had gone. I'm not saying this is what put me off marriage, but it did help.

Then there were my mother's views soundly etched into my thinking: 'Never rely on any man', 'There's no need for a woman to be rushing off into marriage.' I sensed strongly that my mother was suffering from ambition stunted and frustrated by family life, and later, when I had moved happily into acting, the marriages I saw around me – not necessarily in the profession, for those have their own particular problem – were not exactly inspiring.

Marriages between intelligent people who were well aware of its pitfalls generally ended up on the rocks. I thought then and still do, I suppose, that marriage is, amongst other things, a promise to stay with someone for the rest of your life – Till Death Us Do Part. The marriage ceremony is a series of vows, and yet some people go through this ceremony making these promises seven or eight times. How can anyone with half a brain believe Zsa Zsa Gabor, for instance, when she promises Him she will Love and Honour Him until death us do part, knowing she has broken these same promises six or seven times before? I know Miss Gabor is an extreme example, but it seems to me the marriage vows don't mean anything any more. They may as well throw in a few provisos: *so long as he doesn't bore the arse off me*, or, *so long as she doesn't get on my nerves too much*, or, *so long as I don't meet anyone better.* What I'm saying, I suppose, is that the act of getting married doesn't necessarily indicate a maturity or a greater sense of responsibility or even a commitment. The divorce rate proves that.

So I can't bear it when I hear self-righteous little voices saying, 'Umm, but they're not married', or any allusion to Maisie being illegitimate. She was wanted and planned by two people who love and are committed to one another, and her very presence is confirmation that we were right. We might put the legal stamp on it, we might not. That is by the by.

NANNIES

This is a subject that appears to strike despair into the hearts of most working parents. Their faces drop, their voices take on a certain grimness and then come the stories. Tales of stolen duvets, tortured children, ransacked apartments and husband/nanny liaisons. One friend who came round specially to advise me on the subject told me that her first nanny was a nymphomaniac.

'Tell me more,' I urged.

She said that when the nanny was 'getting it' she was as high as a kite, sang constantly in a high-pitched voice, laughed at almost everything and ignored the children. When she wasn't 'getting it' she was extremely depressed, hardly ever washed, didn't speak and ignored the children.

'How did you know it was sexual?' I asked. 'Sounds more like manic depression.'

'Oh, it was sexual, all right,' she said. 'We could tell by her sheets.'

I was appalled. I had visions of my friend and her husband secretly checking the nanny's sheets and saying things like, 'Oh, well, no wonder she's so quiet, the sheets are clean', or 'Oh, well, she should be in a good mood this week, the sheets are as stiff as a board.' I felt quite sorry for the nanny having her sexual privacy charted out on her bedlinen for her employers to peruse whenever they wished.

Anyway, she only lasted a few weeks – apparently it was her BO that eventually drove them to sack her. Then after a couple of good nannies came another humdinger. This one's problems were harder to detect. The baby seemed putty in her hands and always appeared to be asleep if my friend ever popped home during the day. Then the older child, three-year-old Naomi, started reporting incidents of clumsiness on the nanny's part. 'Mummy, Judith fell down the stairs today. It was very funny.' 'Mummy, Judith fell asleep today and nearly dropped Tom on the fire.' 'Mummy, Judith fell over Tom's teddy and sat on the doll's house and the roof's fallen in.' 'Mummy, Tom rolled off the sofa today while Judith was having a bit of a snooze.' 'Mummy, what's a smart arse?'

Finally, Mummy became suspicious enough to make a surprise trip home in the middle of the afternoon. The house was totally silent. Naomi was at playschool, but where were Tom and Judith? Her coat and his pushchair were in the hall, so upstairs Mummy went. Tom was fast asleep in his cot. Judith was in a similar state on her bed and could not be roused. After being pushed, shoved and shouted at she let out the odd, incoherent moan, but then sank back into complete unconsciousness. Suddenly she snapped awake, her eyes bloodshot, her face pale, her speech slow – she had been drinking and had been woken from an alcoholic stupor. Her days were numbered.

On grilling Naomi that evening, Mummy discovered that Judith always went for a bit of a snooze in the afternoon and had threatened Naomi not to tell her mother or the house would be burnt down when everyone was asleep. It also transpired that Tom was given a 'special' bottle in the afternoon to ensure that his sleep coincided with Judith's. Yes, dear reader, he was pissed as well. Judith was duly given her cards and it can't have been more than a couple of weeks later that the house was broken into and ransacked. Jewellery and several first-edition books were stolen and the tin which contained the housekeeping money was taken.

Guess who was arrested a couple of days later in possession of most of the stolen items? It seemed she had a bit of a criminal record which she had omitted to tell them about when she had applied for the job, and her wonderful references had been imaginatively written by herself. The moral being – always check on references.

Another friend, Suzie, swore that her best girls had been untrained. Then I went to stay with her for the weekend. I pulled up on the Friday night in front of the house and was greeted by a tense face at the window. Her current girl, the untrained Nanette, had not yet arrived back from the shops with her son Jake who was five months. It was 6 p.m. and she had left at three for 'an hour or so'.

We went through to the kitchen, which was full of builders and rubble, and sat down for a cup of tea. I asked Suzie what this Nanette was like. She replied that she was the salt of the earth if a little on the scatty side. At this, one of the builders chuckled and muttered something under his breath about her 'having seen a few ceilings'. Suzie rushed to her defence, claiming life hadn't been kind to her – it had given her some hard knocks. 'Yes,' said Trevor, 'most of them to her face.' I was completely fascinated and couldn't wait to meet her.

Two minutes later my wish was granted. Urgent baby cries could be heard coming up the garden path. It sounded like several people were entering the house at once – several people in a scuffle. Keys were dropped two or three times, something hard and heavy crashed to the floor, the front door closed with a house-shaking thud and Jake's screams were now hysterical. Then a huge Mancunian throat opened up and a voice about as soothing as an alarm bell issued forth, 'All right, my darling.' What sounded like several sets of high heels then clattered down the hall. The door opened and in she came, Jake stuffed under one arm, a purple-faced parcel; the other arm clutching a large bag bulging untidily with Jake's belongings. As she entered, several of these fell out.

She was a towering five foot ten with fierce red hair and a dark leathery tan; the latter two qualities were so incongruous that at least one of them had to have come from a bottle. She was wearing a skimpy little tank top which revealed a brown crinkly midriff and a pair of skin-tight jeans. She was about thirty, having seen life. The throat opened again, and all I can say is that those vocal cords must have seen an awful lot of gin and fags to get them to sound like that. Her voice was a mixture of Frank Bruno and Mrs Shufflewick.

'I'm sorry, Suzie, was you worried?' she said, clacking across the quarry tiles and dumping Jake in his mother's anxious arms, 'only I was on me way back, see, and I forgot to pick up Dave's suit from the dry cleaners, so I had to go all the way back again, see, only it's his nephew's stag do tonight and he'll need his best suit to be sick over.' She then let out a deep, mucousy laugh and left. The builder was just shooting me a couple of 'What did I tell you?' looks when she popped her head back round the door and added, with just the teeniest touch of concern, 'Oh, Jakey'll need his tea, Suzie.' With that she was gone.

It was 6.15, he hadn't eaten since one, and, judging from his screams, he thought he was never going to again. Suzie was furious. This was the last straw. 'Feeding the baby is a pretty basic duty – and after what happened last week....'

'What happened last week?' I obliged.

Apparently Suzie was having tea with her excessively camp friend, Kenneth, so Nanette, shocked and rather knocked off balance by Kenneth's outrageous effeminacy and his constant sexual innuendo, decided to take Jake for 'a nice country amble' in his pushchair. Off they set, Nanette aptly dressed in four-inch black patent high heels and skin-tight leggings. About half an hour later the answerphone clicked on in Suzie's hall and an anguished foghorn punctuated by Jake's screams blurted out, 'Suzie, are you there? I've met a nutter.' The voice, hardly needing identification, added, 'It's me, Nanette.'

Suzie rushed to the phone. Nanette, between sobs and expletives and assurances that the screeching Jake was fine, explained, via a torrent of jumbled verbiage, that she was holed up in a nearby cottage, and please could Suzie come and get her.

From what Suzie could make out, Nanette had decided to take a walk down a very lonely, muddy footpath – apparently the sort of place that no one would walk down alone at dusk, let alone a woman in high heels with a baby in a pushchair. After she had got a good 150 yards from the main road and completely out of sight, 'a blooming nutter' leapt from the bushes and dropped his trousers. 'Aw, fuck me!' Nanette had screamed – not perhaps the best thing to have said under the circumstances – and charged off down the path at full pelt, 'the blooming nutter' in hot pursuit, obviously eager to obey her command.

All of a sudden she decided to retrace her steps for the incredible reason that they had dropped Nellie the Elephant. The 'nutter' could not believe his eyes when he saw Nanette turn round and run back in his direction; his luck was in, he instantly stopped and dropped his trousers a second time, obviously thinking she wanted a better look. But, as she got closer to him, and he could see no sign of her slowing down, he must have lost his bottle, for he literally turned tail and ran and, for a brief moment, the tables were turned and she was chasing him. Luckily the poor fellow escaped, but only after tripping over his trousers and falling face down in the mud. 'You bastard!' she cursed after him and then, rescuing

Nellie the Elephant from a puddle, she rushed back to an inconsolable Jake and on to the refuge of a nearby house from which she was now telephoning.

Suzie assured her she would be there within five minutes, and then called the local police station. 'We'll send a car to your address,' an authoritative voice announced. Well, it would be quicker than the bicycle, she thought, knowing that police vehicles at the station numbered one car and the said bicycle, and off she went to the rescue, leaving camp Kenneth to hold the fort.

When she arrived at the cottage there were two very sad creatures waiting for her, both crying and both covered in mud; the pushchair was so caked in the stuff that it looked like something produced by an amateur potter. After thanking the owner of the cottage Suzie installed the weeping duo in the back of the car, Nanette clinging to Jake and Jake in turn clinging to a completely black Nellie the Elephant. And home they sped.

When they got back they found Kenneth serving tea to a policeman who looked about twelve. 'The Force is with us,' Kenneth sneered with a low, throaty hiss. The policeman blushed, and before he could say anything Nanette embarked on her story yet again. It seemed to rush from her as if it had a life of its own, little to do with her, and when it was finished she stood there looking drained and blank.

'Can you give me a description of the man?' the PC asked quietly.

'Ooh yes, was he gorgeous?' enthused Kenneth, ' 'cos if so, officer, I wouldn't mind acting as a decoy.' The policeman's blush deepened to purple as Kenneth sprang from his stool and minced up and down the full length of the kitchen on tiptoe, one hand on his swaying hip, the other suspended limply in space – a bizarre sight since Kenneth was all of six foot two with so much body hair you would think he was going to a fancy dress party. Then, continuing to mince up and down, he acted out the whole scenario, firstly describing what he would wear.

'I would have to look mysterious... a cloak, I think, like the French Lieutenant's Woman. But then... a gust of wind would blow it back to reveal a stunning Basque with fishnets and suspenders. Then I would see him... he would spring out in front of me – tall and handsome. I would scream,' two huge hairy hands delicately cupped his chin in mock horror, 'our eyes would meet, he would slowly unbuckle his studded leather belt. Should I look away? No, I'll be brave. He lets his trousers fall and there it is. . . . ' His look of rapture turned to one of disdain as he eyed the imaginary member. 'Oh, no, dear, I'm sorry. That won't do at all, oh no. Put it under the pillow; we'll smoke it in the morning.'

His act finished, he turned to his little audience for his customary applause. But applause came there none. Suzie was staring at the floor, willing it to open up. Trevor, the builder, who had entered in the middle of the show, was looking at Kenneth as if he was something he had just scraped off his shoe. Nanette just stared, mouth open, like a child at its first visit to a pantomime. Jake was in a similar pose, the mud on his face now beginning to set, and the poor policeman, the colour of a raspberry, quite obviously having never seen anything like Kenneth in his life before, decided to carry on as if the last sixty seconds hadn't happened.

'What was he wearing?' he asked, in a very serious voice.

'A navy blue anorak,' said Nanette, sounding just a little bit wobbly.

'Ooh, and was he about... er six foot, looked like he had just started shaving and blushed a lot?' asked Kenneth excitedly.

'Well, he *was* tall,' said Nanette. 'Why?'

' 'Case solved,' screeched Kenneth, looking pointedly at

the police officer. 'Am I not right in thinking that you are tall, and that the anorak that you are wearing is most definitely navy blue? Where were you at the time of the assault, officer?'

Suzie could take no more. 'Kenneth,' she said, gently, 'let the officer ask his questions.'

'Ooh, all right,' said Kenneth, pretending to be hurt. 'I was only trying to help. And somebody had better wash the mud off this child or we'll end up having to take a hammer and chisel to him.' With that, he scooped baby Jake out of the pushchair and swept out of the room.

Everyone stood there for a couple of seconds, looking awkward. Trevor broke the silence with an acid comment about 'kin' shirt lifters and went on with his work. The poor policeman's interview was now a bit of a shambles, so he decided to go and question the kind cottage owner.

They never caught anyone and Nanette wasn't sacked. That happened a couple of months later when she absent-mindedly left Jake in Safeways and didn't realize it until she had got home. She rushed back to find him in the safe arms of a supervisor, but in her panic to get back to tell Suzie all was well she drove into the back of a bus. No one was hurt, Jake didn't even cry. Suzie did, though. It was her car.

Then, of course, there is the other side of the coin. I have also met several nannies on my travels and their stories are pretty eye-opening too: reports of sexual harassment, sexual jealousy, working virtually twenty-four hours a day for people who did absolutely nothing for their own children, being referred to as 'the girl', not being paid when parents decided to take a holiday. No wonder a lot of nannies lay down so many rules before accepting a job. But all things considered, a nanny is an adult who can get up and leave if she doesn't like her working conditions; the case is not quite the same for an innocent child in the hands of a neglectful, lazy or cruel nanny.

I was lucky. My first nanny started when Maisie was five months and she wasn't a nymphomaniac and wasn't passioned about drink and, most importantly, Maisie adored her.

NOW I UNDERSTAND

Now that Maisie is well and truly here, my relationship with my mother seems to have changed – simply because I have some idea of what being a mother entails. When I think of how much those early weeks took out of me – I never knew what real tiredness was before – and compare it with what my mother must have experienced having my two brothers during the war, with no washing machine, no disposable nappies, no help and little money, it's heartbreaking.

And then there was Grandma. She arrived on the scene just after my eldest brother was born. My grandfather having died, she had sold their farm in the west of Ireland and descended on her eldest daughter to be taken care of in her old age. She had not spoken to my mother for some years – not, in fact, since my mother had announced, by letter, that she was going to marry my father. 'Come home at once,' was the reply. 'A daughter of mine marrying a man in overalls!' she wrote scathingly. My father was a builder and decorator. After the marriage, all communication was severed until the death of my grandfather. Then she arrived, not speaking to my father – he was too far beneath her – and resenting my brother for the simple fact that he was there before she was.

My earliest memories of her, some years after this, were of a tall, rather stately woman, with iron-grey plaited headphones and one yellow tooth in the middle of an otherwise vacant upper set. She was now in her seventies and had suffered two strokes since her arrival. My brothers used to say, 'At the third stroke, she will be seventy-something.' Most of the time she was in a state of utter mental confusion, with only sporadic moments of lucidity. During the latter she would look around her in bewilderment, like someone waking from a nightmare, and cry. The rest of the time she simply did not know what day of the week it was.

My father was constantly being summoned to the local post office at five in the morning to find Grandma completely naked but for a pair of pink interlock-weave bloomers, smelling very strongly of urine and chatting nonsensically away to the weary postmaster and his wife. On seeing my father arrive she would instantly stop talking, give him an imperious look and avert her gaze as if the bad smell was coming from him. There would then be a scuffle as the three of them 'helped' a struggling Grandma into the car. This was a fairly common occurrence, whatever the weather, until one of my brothers pointed out that it was only when she was wearing these particular bloomers that she went wandering the streets in the small hours – so they were hidden. The wandering ceased, and the post office were very grateful until a few weeks later when she formed a similar attachment to an old felt hat. The post office preferred the bloomers.

One of my most vivid memories of Grandma was of a day trip to London to visit an aunt. The M1 had just been built and we were all piled into my father's little grey Ford Esquire Estate with instructions to sit on Grandma should she take a peculiar turn. Expecting the worst, we were pleasantly surprised when she sat there smiling for the entire journey. The only hitch was when she disappeared at one of our frequent toilet stops – these were essential as Grandma was incontinent – and turned up crying twenty minutes later, a pair of soggy bloomers around her ankles. She couldn't find the post office.

The rest of the journey was fine. The visit to my aunt was fine. Everything was fine... until a pigeon shat on Grandma's hat in Trafalgar Square. It reduced us all to uncontrollable mirth, but Grandma didn't even remove her hat. She looked heavenwards, glared angrily at my eldest brother as if he had done it, and then proceeded to lay into him. My parents had to restrain her and she never quite settled down after that.

The journey home was a nightmare. My aunt had given us several magazines for the trip and Grandma slowly ripped them into tiny pieces – the back of the car was like a hamster's nest. Then, after about an hour of this, she announced, 'I'll get up now and make the tea', and started to try and get out of the car. We were hurtling along the M1 at seventy miles an hour. 'For God's sake, sit on her!' my father shouted. We did, and a scuffle then ensued which lasted the remainder of the journey. Tiny scraps of paper flying everywhere, we must have looked from the outside like one of those snowstorm paperweights that had been shaken violently. With great relief, and totally exhausted, we finally reached home. The moment the engine was turned off Grandma instantly became calm. She then slowly looked at each one of us in turn and in a very schoolmistressy voice said, 'We've landed. *Now* are you happy?'

There were several nights when my mother arrived home from work to find the entire contents of the coalhouse on the living room sofa. Grandma sitting exhausted in the middle of it, completely black from head to foot. We, as kids, of course, thought it was great fun, though Grandma didn't help our social lives very much. A couple of my friends refused to come to our house at all because not only were they frightened of Grandma but they didn't like the smell. I was so used to it I didn't really notice it, but any unsuspecting visitor sitting in Grandma's chair was in for a shock. It was like sitting on a sponge and squelched with wee-wee at the slightest pressure. It was also next to the fire. The other abiding image of Grandma was turning around from the tea table to see her happily tucking into a boiled egg with a huge pair of coal tongs.

But even more strongly etched in my memory is my poor mother's weary face as she uttered the words, 'May the great God look to me.' My mother died this year, before I had the chance to tell her that Now I Understand.